# TOGETHER

## BUILDING BETTER, STRONGER COMMUNITIES

Working Draft, Spring 2021

David Mathews

Cousins Research Group, The Kettering Foundation

*Together: Building Better, Stronger Communities* is published by the Kettering Foundation Press. The interpretations and conclusions contained in this publication, unless expressly stated to the contrary, represent the views of the author and not necessarily those of the Kettering Foundation, its directors, or its officers.


Editors: Paloma Dallas and Lisa Boone-Berry
Copy Editor: Ellen Dawson-Witt
Design and Production: Laura Halsey

## ABOUT THE KETTERING FOUNDATION

The Kettering Foundation is a nonprofit operating foundation rooted in the American tradition of cooperative research. Kettering's primary research question is, What does it take to make democracy work as it should? Kettering's research is distinctive because it is conducted from the perspective of citizens and focuses on what people can do collectively to address problems affecting their lives, their communities, and their nation. The foundation seeks to identify and address the challenges to making democracy work as it should through interrelated program areas that focus on citizens, communities, and institutions. The foundation collaborates with an extensive network of community groups, professional associations, researchers, scholars, and citizens around the world. Established in 1927 by inventor Charles F. Kettering, the foundation is a 501(c)(3) organization that does not make grants but engages in joint research with others.

## ABOUT THE COUSINS RESEARCH GROUP

The Cousins Research Group is one of the internal research divisions of the Kettering Foundation. Named for Norman Cousins, a leading American journalist and Kettering Foundation board member from 1967 to 1987, the group synthesizes different lines of study into books and articles and also proposes new lines of inquiry. The central focus for the group, as for the foundation, is on the role that citizens play in a democracy. Within the Cousins Research Group, there are a number of "departments." One looks at the effect of federal policy on citizens, communities, and democracy itself, with an eye for implications on the relationship between citizens and government today. Another, the political anthropology and etymology group, examines the origins of human history for clues to how human beings collectively make decisions. A core group is also asked to prepare our research for publication. This group regularly writes for Kettering's periodicals, *Connections*, the *Kettering Review*, and the *Higher Education Exchange*, as well as for other publications.

Print ISBN: 978-1-945577-57-4
PDF ISBN: 978-1-945577-58-1
Ebook ISBN: 978-1-945577-59-8
Library of Congress Control Number: 2021936705

# TABLE OF CONTENTS

# INTRODUCTION

This book is about our communities and how much we need them to work at their best in today's political environment. That environment is extremely challenging, to say the least, and is likely to remain so for some time. In meeting these challenges, I believe communities that work democratically work best and become stronger. A democracy engages the energies of everyone, and everyone is needed to combat today's problems.[1]

crisis
Global
'CRITICAL'
Keep up self-isolation policy
blame
closures
enforce
COVID-19 PANIC
CORONAVIRUS OUTBREAK
isolated
essential
entire world
save
give food
virus
lay-off
self-isolation
border

## CRISIS UPON CRISIS

In 2020, the United States was hit by a tsunami of cascading crises: The COVID-19 pandemic. The resulting economic meltdown. Protests sparked by the death of George Floyd and others. Some believed that our country was in serious trouble because it had lost its moral compass. Others talked with just as much concern about justice denied and the growing disparity in incomes. These crises came on top of a decades-old weakening of democracy. Major governing institutions from the legislative, executive, and even judicial branches of government had lost much of the confidence that citizens once had in them. Nongovernmental institutions and the media suffered a similar loss.[2] Trust in the facts that experts offered was in short supply.

Research suggests that the forces driving these changes in the political environment in many democratic countries were coming from people's long-building resentment with the way governing institutions saw them (as incompetent) and often treated them (with disdain).[3] A Kettering Foundation report, *With the People*, discusses these forces in more detail and suggests there may be better ways of responding to this lost institutional legitimacy than the current attempts to engage citizens.

Responding effectively, even talking together constructively, was often blocked by political polarization and social divisiveness. Words became weapons. Our country appeared to be approaching the level of conflict that Thomas Hobbes described as a war of "every man against every man." He called that the worst of all worlds.[4] Even when people agreed that something was terribly wrong, there was no agreement about what exactly it was or what should be done.

The good news is that Americans agreed on one thing: There was far too much divisiveness. And people were joining forces across dividing lines to help one another when natural or human-made disasters struck. At the neighborhood and grassroots level, citizens increasingly came together as humans have always done instinctively when faced with danger. Furthermore, studies showed there is more common ground underneath the policy disputes than has been recognized.[5]

Communities had been getting more favorable attention before these crises hit. We were finally addressing an imbalance that public administration scholar George Frederickson pointed out years ago. In the 20th century, he noted, we were occupied with building larger institutions and systems while neglecting communities. The 2020 crises showed, however, that local politics suffered from many of the same problems that plagued politics at the national level—albeit to a lesser degree. While local institutions benefit from closer proximity to citizens, some of them suffered from distressing turmoil. Churches, for instance, reported polarized congregations.[6]

Despite this vulnerability, however, there has been a greater recognition of the essential role communities play in protecting our health, educating our children, caring for those in need, and developing economic resilience. We also have become more aware that communities are the homes of democracy. They are where people can participate directly in self-government through civic associations, as well as citizen boards and councils.

**WE ALSO HAVE BECOME MORE AWARE THAT COMMUNITIES ARE THE HOMES OF DEMOCRACY. THEY ARE WHERE PEOPLE CAN PARTICIPATE DIRECTLY IN SELF-GOVERNMENT.**

## WHO WANTS ME TO KNOW THIS?

Now, before saying more, I should introduce myself and the Kettering Foundation. I'll do this because, in presenting research, we were once asked, "Who wants me to know this?" I thought that was a good question. Ever since, I have tried to answer it up front.

This book is based on studies from the Kettering Foundation. Despite having "foundation" in its title, Kettering is a nonpartisan, not-for-profit research institute that studies how to make democracy work as it should. We don't do research *on* others but rather *with* them. These other parties include a broad array of organizations that work directly with people in communities. They include religious congregations, civic organizations, grantmaking foundations, governments, schools and colleges, and the media. Since we don't give grants, Kettering doesn't fund what these other parties do. Instead, the foundation learns from their experiences and, in return, shares what it has learned from its previous research.[7]

[Kettering is still trying to determine how best to describe what it is learning, which is why this book is called a "working draft." Throughout the book, you'll see brackets like this one with our questions about other ways to present the research.]

I am particularly interested in communities because I am from a small, rural one. My wife, Mary, and I still keep a home there. Prior to my coming to Kettering, I was a history professor, a university president, and a cabinet secretary in the Ford administration (the US Department of Health, Education, and Welfare). I am a nonpartisan independent, gardener, parent, grandparent, and, recently, a great-grandparent.

I have pleasant memories of growing up in a family of farmers and teachers but realize that I have to be cautious about romanticizing small town life. Not everyone where I lived had the same experiences I did. However, I'm not alone in my attraction to these little communities. Nelle, a friend and neighbor in adjoining Monroe County, liked to exchange stories about our towns every time Mary and I visited. Nelle, aka Nelle Harper Lee, turned her stories into *To Kill a Mockingbird*. Nothing I have written comes close to that. But I don't have to worry about movie rights to what I publish.

## THE CHALLENGES

So much that we care about—the education of young people, our health, our social well-being, even the vitality of the economy—is linked to the strength of our communities. Although pleased to see that communities are now being recognized, I have to remind myself that they are plagued by the same maladies that affect all humankind. They can be parochial and immobilized by friction between political cliques. They struggle to overcome crime and entrenched poverty. They can be engulfed by violence. Sometimes local governments may be less than effective. And a community's economy can be crippled when an established industry abruptly leaves or fails. Young people often want to get out of their hometowns as fast as they can and never return. So much for romanticism.

In spite of the rediscovery of the importance of communities, their challenges are daunting, and citizens have an especially critical role to play in meeting them. (By "citizens," I mean anyone who works with others to make the place they call home better.) The big question about citizens is whether they have the ability, resources, and political will to shoulder the responsibility of citizenship. Based on our research, we think they do, although we are quite aware of the many arguments to the contrary. This book will consider both sides of the argument over the competence of citizens.

The problems communities face aren't all the same. Some are easy to see and can be easily remedied: Fix the potholes! Others lie below the surface and don't have obvious solutions. Such problems have "wicked" characteristics. Strategies for countering these problems have to engage citizens from every sector of the community because the problems have multiple sources located in different parts of a town. Combating problems with these characteristics is made even more difficult by structural fault lines in the social order and economic system. Discrimination is often cited as an example. The inequitable distribution of goods produced by collective efforts is another.

To better understand the problem-solving strategies of communities, my colleagues and I looked more closely into areas like civic leadership and public engagement. The usual ways that communities solve problems are fine for the usual problems, but not for combating the ones with wicked characteristics. This book discusses what an effective community strategy would have to do in order to counter this wickedness and be effective over the long term.

The need for ongoing, community-wide citizen engagement is usually a special concern for those leading problem-solving initiatives. When the outpouring of people helping disaster victims fades away, volunteers go back home. Community leaders continue to organize meetings, but only a handful of folks attend. Leaders ask for volunteers, and the same thing happens. Many people appear to be apathetic about the well-being of their community. And this lack of engagement frustrates those in leadership roles.

In our research, we took an especially careful look at the apparently apathetic. We wondered if "apathy" is really the right diagnosis for the people who don't participate in civic projects. Do they have different perceptions of the community or different concerns from those acting as leaders? And if that is the case, what can be done to engage enough people from across a community to respond to the problems that have multiple sources?

Problems of any kind are seldom dealt with effectively without new insights into what the problems really are. Such insights rarely drop out of the clouds or appear as flashes of lightning. Often, they are stimulated by what we see other people doing as they approach a familiar problem from a different perspective. How might these insights occur more often in our communities? This book devotes a great deal of attention to that question.

I don't know of any exact science of communities. I'm not sure there is one. There are materials on group processes that community organizations can use, which might be helpful in organizing a meeting. Problems with wicked characteristics, however, are unlikely to be solved by any single meeting or intervention. They recur, particularly when they are about relationships, which have to be constantly restructured to meet ever-changing circumstances. So communities have to develop long-term strategies. After all, democracy itself is a journey, not a destination.

## CREATING A LEARNING COMMUNITY

Because democracy is a journey, there is no detailed road map, just a few guideposts. Those who make the journey have to call on their inventiveness because much of the road has to be made by walking it.

Communities where people are learning together are better at adapting to changes in circumstances that they can't control. They are more likely to keep the things they want to preserve and to change the things that need to change.

## STARTING WITH A "BOOK CLUB"

Many books are to be read in the comfort of an easy chair or at a desk. *Together* isn't. It is written to be read one chapter at a time and then discussed by any group of people who want to come together to better understand how they can contribute to making their community a better place to live, raise a family, and work. This book is designed to be read TOGETHER. That can be the first step to creating a learning community.

To help a group of readers share what they have learned about their community, the last chapter, chapter 7, ends with blank pages. This isn't a printing error; there is a reason. We thought these groups might want to talk about what they were reading and make a record of anything they thought applied to their communities. Maybe they discovered some things they hadn't noticed before or came to new insights. Perhaps they did some experiments and needed an account of what happened. Since Kettering has no way of knowing in advance what readers will learn, I couldn't write the final chapter.

Because the last chapter offers some suggestions about how you or your group might use the empty pages, you may want to read the introductory section of chapter 7 before you read chapter 1.

ARCHIVES OF THE UNITED STATES OF AMERICA

## CHAPTER ONE

# REDISCOVERING COMMUNITIES

I want to say more about the renewed interest in communities and why they are so important in areas from health care to economic development. And I'll make the case that what happens in communities, in the final analysis, depends to a large extent on what everyday citizens do.

## WHAT COMMUNITIES DO

Scholarly articles, books, and news stories have been filled with encouraging stories about neighborhoods, "ordinary" people, and what is happening locally. "Think Locally, Act Locally" was a headline in the *New York Times* book review section.[8] *Times* columnist David Brooks reported on small towns that are being revived.[9] Another article in the *Atlantic* by James Fallows cited a poll indicating that 70 percent of

Americans trusted their local governments. Fallows used this to argue that in "underpublicized ways . . . America [is] moving forward locally and regionally."[10] In 2018, he and Deborah Fallows published a book on this same theme.[11] Communities, including those with diverse populations, were given credit for the "reinvention of America." And columnist Thomas Friedman concluded that "American Politics Can Still Work: From the Bottom Up."[12]

Despite their optimism, I am sure none of these writers are oblivious to the failure of many communities to reach their potential or solve their many problems. Still, against the backdrop of what was happening nationally, local politics looked much better. But take away that comparison and the warts are visible. Problems like the hyperdivisiveness that erodes a sense of community are as contagious as a virus.

In 2020, some of the local responses to the coronavirus pandemic showed that community action is essential. Before long, however, there were troubling events in cities that dampened any assumption that local towns and neighborhoods were "paradise."

Sounding a cautious note, Brian Adams, a political science professor at San Diego State University, has argued that despite being closer to the people, local governments may not be that different from their state and federal counterparts. In fact, he has found Americans who don't find local governments responsive to people's concerns, but rather see them as dominated by corrupt elites. On the other hand, an April 2020 Pew Research survey finds that 74 percent found local governmental responses to the pandemic to be "about right" and 72 percent thought state governmental responses to be "about right."[13]

## SMALL IS BEAUTIFUL[14]

What exactly do these studies and articles mean by "communities"? Some go back to the word itself, which means to share with and care for others. This sense of community binds us together when disasters strike. The more typical meaning of community has to do with local institutions, such as municipal governments and chapters of major nonprofit organizations. These institutions, including businesses and schools, are certainly the visible features of communities. Yet small associations and informal grassroots groups are proving to be as—and in some cases more—crucial in determining what happens in a community. Peter Block, who has written a great deal about communities, believes small groups are essential because they allow everyone to be heard and depend on everyone to act. Found in neighborhoods, they are indispensable bridges between individuals and the larger community. Linked together, they create civic infrastructure and generate civic energy.[15]

**SMALL ASSOCIATIONS AND INFORMAL GRASSROOTS GROUPS ARE PROVING TO BE AS—AND IN SOME CASES MORE—CRUCIAL IN DETERMINING WHAT HAPPENS IN A COMMUNITY.**

I believe Block is right about small groups. Still, I'm realistic about the limited resources many people and communities have. My own small community in Alabama is hardly a boomtown. Yet it, and most other small communities, even impoverished ones, have assets that can be tapped. These assets are in the experiences and skills people have, as well as in the ability of citizens to cooperate and join forces. The associations people form, John McKnight has long argued, are themselves resources.[16]

## WHERE COMMUNITIES MATTER

The rediscovery of the importance of communities isn't just a fantasy or limited to a few cases. Even if communities aren't perfect, what we have learned about what they can do—if they work as they should—still stands.

### *IN HEALTH*

Communities rely on hospitals, clinics, and medical professionals to care *for* us. Yet only the citizenry in a community can organize the human ability to care *about* us, which is a potent "medicine." A growing health literature speaks to the role a community can play in people's physical well-being. And it is now widely recognized that, in addition to family and friends, larger "networks of nurture" organized by communities can be a significant force in combating the behavioral problems that contribute to many illnesses. This has been demonstrated in research done for the national Centers for Disease Control and Prevention, which shows that community care can reduce the incidence of heart disease, strokes, and lung cancer.[17]

**IT IS NOW WIDELY RECOGNIZED THAT, IN ADDITION TO FAMILY AND FRIENDS, LARGER "NETWORKS OF NURTURE" ORGANIZED BY COMMUNITIES CAN BE A SIGNIFICANT FORCE IN COMBATING THE BEHAVIORAL PROBLEMS THAT CONTRIBUTE TO MANY ILLNESSES.**

Organizing the care given by individuals into a collective form (e.g., a group that walks together each afternoon) is a civic act that concentrates the power of caring about others. Communities can promote these associations, which can then multiply and form influential norms—accepted ways of behaving. Communities with norms promoting healthy behaviors are healthy communities.

When he became ill, Lyndon Johnson's father defended his decision to go back to his community by explaining, "They know when you are sick and care if you die."[18] This wasn't just sentimentality but rather a recognition of the power in people caring about people, which can augment what professionals provide.

I like the insights of Ronald Heifetz, a physician turned scholar, who teaches at Harvard's Kennedy School of Government. He explains why behavior-linked medicine is now being recognized. Heifetz knows from his background as a physician that there are significant differences in types of medical problems and that each makes different demands on doctors and patients. These problems range from those that are routine and can be cured by a physician to more serious ones for which the diagnosis isn't clear-cut and medical interventions alone aren't enough. Think of the difference between a broken arm and diabetes; there is a technical remedy for the former, but not the latter. For problems like diabetes, the patient and physician have to combine forces. The same is true of other medical problems. Professionals, clinics, and hospitals are necessary, yet, by themselves, not sufficient.[19]

Let me also introduce you to Dr. Sandral Hullett, who was a physician in the rural town of Eutaw, Alabama. There, health statistics were alarming for diseases like breast cancer. One reason was that few women were getting checkups. So, the cancers were growing and becoming life threatening. Dr. Hullett was aware of research showing that community deliberations on how to solve problems influence the way the people who participate behave. Making decisions with others about how to respond to diseases has more effect on behaviors than admonitions or even better medical information.[20] So Dr. Hullett decided to test this finding. She encouraged deliberative forums in her community on what should be done to combat breast cancer.

In these forums, people considered a variety of options for solving the problem, including some that Dr. Hullett didn't particularly care for. Even though there was not full agreement on which of the options was best for everyone, just being in the deliberations changed behavior. There was a 20 percent increase in mammograms in one year. Deliberating, she found, also had other beneficial side effects. Participants in the forums began to associate across racial and economic lines much more freely. Later, many expressed interest in organizing similar forums on prostate cancer. Dr. Hullett's findings matched those of Kurt Lewin's earlier research on the effects of collective decision-making.[21]

### *IN SOCIAL WELL-BEING*

The role of communities in health is only one of the many roles that they can play. I once visited a neighborhood where almost everything that could fall down had fallen down; crumbling, boarded buildings lined littered streets. There I met a group of elderly citizens from as many diverse backgrounds as I have ever encountered. We had to pray in three languages just to eat lunch. During the meal, I was seated next to a lady named Sallie Jackson, who, along with others, had rallied the people in that area to combine their own resources with resources from the federal and state governments to create a partnership that was transforming their blighted neighborhood into a community of strength and vitality. Mrs. Jackson was one of the citizens I was talking about when I said that what happens in a community is determined by what citizens do, or don't do. Her history is instructive; it shows the power that can come from working with people.

Mrs. Jackson was the kind of person usually classed as "ordinary," yet what she was doing as president of the governing council for her neighborhood association was exceptional, even though her background was far from privileged. Born in McDuffie County, Georgia, she left school in the sixth grade to help her family work its tenant farm. At 21, she moved to South Carolina; there she met her husband, Hilliary Jackson, who worked on a highway crew. They married in 1933 and migrated to Philadelphia, where Hilliary was employed by a construction company. Until 1954, when she developed acute bursitis, Sallie had worked as a seamstress. Her story wasn't unlike that of many of the other "ordinary" people having lunch the day I visited. Together, they had created a community that was its own social service center.

This group of senior citizens did things that most of us only dream of doing. They crossed racial, ethnic, and religious barriers that had been considered insurmountable. They fought against an urban decay that has defeated the best public planners. Most significant, they created an environment of warmth, friendliness, and caring that renewed all who were in it. Sure, they had outside resources, but they were not done unto—they did. Theirs was not a bootstraps alone story. Sallie and her neighbors didn't see themselves as merely the objects of others' interventions; they were self-empowering agents doing "their thing."

**THE WORK OF SCHOOLS IS TEACHING, WHICH IS PART, THOUGH NOT ALL, OF EDUCATING. AND WHILE MOST FORMAL INSTRUCTION MAY BE LEFT LARGELY TO PROFESSIONALS, COMMUNITIES CAN, AND HAVE ALWAYS, EDUCATED BY USING LOCAL RESOURCES AND OTHER LOCAL EDUCATING INSTITUTIONS.**

### *IN EDUCATION*

While the connection between communities and health, as well as social well-being, is usually recognized, the role of communities in education has been contested. Yet schools can benefit enormously from what communities do to help prepare the next generation of young people for the future. The work of schools is teaching, which is part, though not all, of educating. And while most formal instruction may be left largely to professionals, communities can, and have always, educated by using local resources and other local educating institutions. This was documented in Lawrence Cremin's Pulitzer Prize-winning history of education in America.[22] Cremin saw educating as any sustained effort to transmit, evoke, or acquire knowledge, values, attitudes, skills, or sensibilities.[23] He identified a variety of educating institutions other than schools to show that the country has long educated through families, faith-based institutions, libraries, museums, benevolent societies, youth groups, agricultural fairs, radio and television stations, newspapers, and military organizations.[24] What children learn in educating institutions other than schools can reinforce what happens in classrooms. Many community institutions like agricultural fairs and local newspapers that publish articles by students provide a valuable, real-world context for learning.[25] (The use of community resources to educate was illustrated when the coronavirus pandemic closed schools.)

I have been quite impressed by what John (Jack) Shelton has shown about how community resources educate through a program called PACERS, which assists rural schools. My favorite example comes from a PACERS project in Coffeeville, Alabama, which is near where I grew up. In this case, the community provided a unique resource, its own history, to augment what the school was teaching. Old-timers came to the school to tell children stories of what the community was like when they were young. Then those stories were turned into songs by the school and sung back to the community. Coffeeville was an educating community.[26]

PACERS has also used things that citizens have built to educate: solar homes, greenhouses, fish ponds, as well as local newsrooms turned into "classrooms."[27] The citizens who organize these initiatives pull their community together around a project and bring young people into it as a means of enriching their education.[28] This is community organizing that uses the resources of the community to educate.

**EDUCATORS WHO AREN'T TEACHERS:** Many people who educate aren't teachers by profession. This is significant because the prevailing assumption is that only professionals can teach. The educating citizens do has been documented by Pat Harbour in her study of community educators.[29] Another example comes from Kentucky. Bruce Mundy, who worked in the teen center of a health department, worried about youngsters who came to his after-school program. He said, "I've got kids who can't read. To me, that is a crisis." But he did more than teach reading; he provided a context to stimulate learning. There was a lot of trash around housing projects that had recently been razed, so Bruce got his kids to start a cleanup. They also hacked away at the 10-foot weeds surrounding an old cemetery, which proved to be a valuable historical site. The youngsters found the gravesites of veterans of the Civil War and winning jockeys in the Kentucky Derby, many of whom were African Americans. The students researched those names and got the (now pristine) site on the National Register of Historic Places. "'Scuse me while I teach history!" Bruce joked.[30]

I heard still another story about educators who aren't teachers from Wiley Mullins, a businessman who explained how his own love of learning began when he was sitting in the barber's chair in his hometown, a rather unlikely site for education. The barber told parents that if they brought their youngsters in on Saturdays, he would cut their hair for a dollar. When the children walked into the barbershop, there were six boxes of books lined up along the wall, each marked with numbers, 1 through 6. As they were sitting down to get their hair cut, the barber would ask, "What grade are you in?" If the youngster said, "first grade," the barber then would respond, "I want you to go over and get a book out of box 1. While I cut your hair, read it to me." He would do the same for the other five grades. Here was a barber encouraging reading; his barbershop was an educational institution. And he isn't the only barber who has done something similar.[31]

**HERE WAS A BARBER ENCOURAGING READING; HIS BARBERSHOP WAS AN EDUCATIONAL INSTITUTION. AND HE ISN'T THE ONLY BARBER WHO HAS DONE SOMETHING SIMILAR.**

The conclusion of Wiley's story is even more remarkable. Years later, he returned home and ran into the wife of the barber, now a widow. He told her how important his experience in the barbershop had been for him and other kids in the community. She said, "Yes. My husband loved to hear children read. Did you know that he couldn't read himself?"

Other community-based enterprises have formed alliances with schools and become educating institutions. For instance, in Kentucky, a farm for retired racehorses has been used to supplement classroom instruction.[32] Nearly everybody in Lexington loves horse racing. And some of these horse lovers were distressed when they found that, after winners of the Kentucky Derby had passed their prime, some went to the glue factory. So, people started buying these champions and putting them on a farm they named "Old Friends." Then, at the invitation of the farm, the principal of an alternative school began sending students to work with the horses. Along with that work, the school added a little instruction. Biology probably wasn't so formidable in the context of racehorses. Kids who had no interest in the classroom began to learn.[33]

The city of Chattanooga, Tennessee, took into consideration all of a community's educating institutions when a local civic group identified the many places where young people could learn something useful. The group produced a map showing all those educating institutions. They included, but were not confined to, libraries, museums, television stations, and, of course, schools. Businesses, for instance, taught in much the way craft guilds did centuries ago, that is, through the apprentice system. Each educating institution brought its own unique array of resources to bear on education. For example, teaching mathematics and science, in all their complexity, can benefit from resources that aren't found in schools. A zoo's staff can teach zoology. A grocery store provides a practical context for teaching math; a builder can teach from a knowledge of materials.[34]

**THE COMMUNITY ITSELF AS THE EDUCATOR:** What stands in the way of schools taking advantage of the education provided by people who aren't professional educators? Thinking of the community itself as an educator, with the

schools playing a supporting role, might encourage a closer alignment between what happens in community educating institutions (like barbershops and horse farms) and schools. Creating this alignment would mean adapting what schools do to mesh with the educating that a community does.

One of the boldest arguments for treating the community as the primary educating institution is found in the work of Edmund Gordon, professor emeritus at Columbia's Teachers College.[35] He made a strong case for concentrating on communities rather than just on schools to improve education. Gordon believed in the importance of what he called "intellective competence," which is "the competence to use one's intellect to meet the requirements of living." Communities are the schools for developing these abilities, he said, because the "texts" are in the lives of the people who live in them.[36]

Seeing the community as the primary educator has implications for the way communities are understood. It suggests that they should do more than provide services and protect the physical well-being of residents. Communities, in the richest sense, are responsible for providing people with opportunities to develop to their fullest potential. And that requires them to educate.

Projects using a community strategy to educate have been found in St. Louis Park, Minnesota, and Albion, Michigan. In both cases, people and organizations from across the community worked together to make the education of children a priority. I hasten to emphasize that people working together to educate doesn't have to be highly organized. Informal initiatives are fine. Living rooms and kitchen tables have been wellsprings for all kinds of learning.

The more people talk about "education broadly," and not just teaching alone, the more they may turn their attention to their communities and all their educating institutions. No one explained that better than a Baton Rouge resident who reasoned there should be "a community strategy, not a school strategy, for educating every single child."[37]

Another way that communities educate is through social norms, which either value education or don't. In one community, the norm was for everyone to do what they could to help educate young people. That attitude helped develop a culture supportive of learning. This kind of culture is a community resource.

To see the community itself as an educator in no way detracts from the importance of schools. I want to make this clear because seeing "education" as more than "school" has prompted strong pushback in the past. Throughout our history, schools have been instruments for our country's objectives—from advancing equity to defending the nation against technological rivals. Schools were so important that early settlers on the frontier often built the first ones themselves. And the community wasn't just "involved" in the schools; the two were inseparable. Different Americans had different reasons for supporting public schools, but by the 19th century most had come to much the same conclusion—public schools were an essential public good. That was the basis for devoting tax dollars to education.

### *IN ECONOMIC DEVELOPMENT*

What about the economy? Is that just a matter of labor, capital, and technology? And is it the sole province of state and national governments because they set the policies that influence economic development? It turns out an economy is made up of not only capital, labor, and technology. Communities also belong on that list. The key variables that determine a local community's economy are greatly affected by what a community's citizenry does or doesn't do. In communities that thrive, citizens have developed the habits of working together; these habits transfer to the factory floor and to corporate offices.

**COMMUNITY-BASED ECONOMIC DEVELOPMENT:** A great deal of what Kettering has learned about communities' roles in the economy has come from reports by economic development veterans like J. Mac Holladay. In *Economic and Community Development*, he argues, "Economic development is a part of a larger, more important process involving and reflecting the life and activity of the community."[38] That life—the civic life of a community—forms around projects that citizens carry out with other citizens: organizing youth development programs to reinforce schools, creating support groups for those with chronic illnesses, expanding the scope of the local historical society to include everyone's history. Many of these projects appear to have little to do with the economy, and yet they are crucial. I suspect that what people do in these projects is less important than the habits of working together that they develop.

**WHAT PEOPLE DO IN THESE PROJECTS IS LESS IMPORTANT THAN THE HABITS OF WORKING TOGETHER THAT THEY DEVELOP.**

**THE WORKPLACE AS A COMMUNITY:** In writing about the creation of prosperity, Francis Fukuyama describes the "community" that formed in an industry, which had implications for the surrounding community. He found that some economic actors, like the Toyota Motor Corporation, developed a community of mutual trust in their factories. Workers supported one another and the businesses flourished, even when economic conditions weren't good. These results weren't because of rules or policies, but rather they came from a culture that promoted workplace solidarity.[39] The managers and workers who lived in residential communities took this culture with them when they went home from their jobs. It stands to reason that if the culture in those communities of place promoted the same values prized in the work culture, it would be reinforcing. And that would pay off both in social and in economic terms.

There is a difference between a community as a group of diverse people drawn together for whatever serves their common good and a company, which is a group of certain people brought together for one specific purpose. Nonetheless, Fukuyama shows that what I said about civic skills and habits of working together transferring to the factory floor can be true in reverse.

**CHANGING THE ECONOMY, AGAIN:** Sociologist Vaughn Grisham Jr. has done an excellent, and very thorough, case study of Tupelo, Mississippi, about how a community changed its economy repeatedly as circumstances changed. Initially, Tupelo focused on dairy farms. Later, in the mid-1950s, furniture making became a significant part of the economy. Then, as community leaders saw manufacturing beginning to decline, they shifted their focus to education, eventually leading to the opening of the Tupelo branch of the University of Mississippi. An educated workforce, they reasoned, would be better able to respond to more changes in the economy.[40]

Tupelo was once called the poorest town in the poorest state in the country. The only reason you might have heard of it is that it was Elvis Presley's hometown. Now it is known for citizen-based efforts that turned rural poverty into regional prosperity. Grisham provides a detailed, longitudinal study of this transformation, which began very simply when smaller, rural settlements around Tupelo decided to initiate projects to solve local problems.

Tupelo benefited from the example set by people in the rural areas around the town. They didn't ask outsiders to take care of their problems. They asked themselves what *they* could do to make the places where they lived better. Those in one rural neighborhood diverted water that threatened their roads while those in another painted their school building. What people did wasn't as important as the fact that they did it *themselves*. Citizens acting to solve problems year after year eventually changed the political culture of the entire Tupelo region. The new culture reinforced a sense of local responsibility and an appreciation for what people could do by working together. Of course, outside assistance was needed in some situations. Yet that comes more often when there is a local initiative to build on. And because of the local initiative, outside help is more effective. The secret of Tupelo's success wasn't in some master plan. It was in asking and answering one question every year: What can we do to make our community a better place to live?[41]

## THE UNIQUE ROLE OF CITIZENS

Not only is much of what communities have done accomplished by people working together, *some* of what has been achieved could have been done only by citizens. I realize that saying that there are some things only citizens can do usually prompts a rebuttal. And I'll try to respond.

### ONLY CITIZENS

One way that the work citizens do with citizens is unique is that it's unlike the work done by institutions and their professionals. People don't identify problems in expert terms: They take into account how their experiences helped them see what was most valuable and should be held dear when deciding on how to combat problems. People also have access to local knowledge that comes from years of direct experience with problems. And the options for actions to solve these problems go beyond the things that can be done by institutions. Citizens act through the civic associations they form and through their families and friends. Furthermore, citizens don't make decisions about which options are best using institutional methods, such as cost-benefit analysis. And the resources citizens draw on, such as personal talents and collective experiences, are different from institutional resources. Citizens also organize their work less bureaucratically than institutions do. Even when the work institutions do is the same as the work done by citizens, people working with people has a distinctive quality. My neighbors may do what a construction crew does to keep our lane clean. Yet, that the people living around me work together in the clean-up builds a stronger sense of community.[42]

The contributions that citizens can make to community institutions are also distinctive. Governing councils and agencies can't create their own legitimacy. They can't, on their own, define their purposes or set the standards by which they will operate. Governments, in particular, can't sustain decisions that citizens are unwilling to support.

Governments can build common highways, but not common ground. Neither can institutions do the civic work required to complement their work and that of their professionals. Furthermore, institutions—even the most powerful—can't generate the political will required to keep a community moving ahead to combat difficult problems. Will is essential in attacking those problems that grow out of a lack of community and then further destroy community. Finally, large institutions alone, governmental or nongovernmental, can't create a democratic citizenry capable of governing itself.

**AN EXAMPLE, SURVIVING DISASTERS:** Governing is solving problems, and a democratic citizenry does that by working together voluntarily. Research has found that in the first days after a natural or human-made disaster strikes, survival depends largely on people helping people. One study concludes that "successful remedies and recovery for community-wide disasters are neither conceived nor implemented solely by trained emergency personnel, nor are they confined to preauthorized procedures." Rather, "family members, friends, coworkers, neighbors, and strangers who happen to be in the vicinity often carry out search and rescue activities and provide medical aid before police, fire, and other officials even arrive on the scene."[43] Disasters reveal what only citizens can do. We saw that begin to happen when coping with the multiple crises in 2020.

**ANOTHER EXAMPLE, COMBATING CRIME:** Studies on combating crime also show the unique role that groups of citizens can play. This was evident in a study of why some cities were able to lower their crime rates when others couldn't.[44]

Municipal crime rates in the United States reached historic lows in 2014, but this wasn't true for all cities. Why the difference? Part of the reduction came from reforms in policing, yet that, by itself, wasn't the decisive factor.[45] A study by Patrick Sharkey finds that "ordinary citizens" made the difference using the civic associations they formed. "Mobilization against violence . . . was driven by residents and local organizations to retake parks, alleyways, [and] city blocks."[46] Interestingly, benefits from the local organizations that citizens form come from more than specific projects directed at preventing violence. Citing a group called Concerned Citizens of South Central Los Angeles, Emily

Badger reports that these projects evolve so that, "in creating playgrounds, they enabled parents to better monitor their children. In connecting neighbors, they improved the capacity of residents to control their streets. In forming after-school programs, they offered alternatives to crime."[47] These are lessons to keep in mind when the issues have to do with public safety and justice.

The negative energy coming from fear, frustration, and anger turns positive as citizens join forces in work. The change isn't just the result of producing tangibles like playgrounds or after-school programs; it's brought about by the added value that comes from the human touch of the neighbors who created the programs and playgrounds.

## COMING UP NEXT

As appealing as the cases cited in this chapter are, they won't remove doubts about the ability of regular folks to govern themselves, even in a country where the agencies of representative government do a great deal of the governing. Serious obstacles stand in the way, many having to do with the perception that people aren't up to meeting the demands of active citizenship. Citizens really can't make much of a difference outside of voting, or so the argument goes.

Chapter 2 looks at these doubts without dismissing them out of hand. Many are backed by valid reasons. This next chapter will also report on how citizens have responded to these challenges.

## CHAPTER TWO

# CAN CITIZENS REALLY MAKE A DIFFERENCE?

As you have read, this book is saying that for communities to work as they should, a great deal depends on the citizenry. That claim usually stops the conversation because of serious doubts about citizens, so I want to speak to these reservations before going on. Doubts that citizens can or will do all that self-government requires go back to the dawn of democracy. The examples I have given in the first chapter are written off as occasional exceptions.

Today, those who question the competence of "The People" range from heads of major institutions to experts in professional fields to civic leaders in communities. Even citizens themselves question their own political effectiveness. At best, critics say, people can be voters and responsible consumers of government services—provided they are properly educated. But that's about all.

Frankly, there are reasons for the pessimism about citizens. The voice of The People isn't infallible. And there are many cases where sound judgments by citizens have been precluded because of hasty reactions and popular prejudices.

## THE CHALLENGES

This chapter concentrates on serious obstacles that contribute to the perception that most citizens really can't make a significant difference. But it does add a few more cases showing how people deal with the obstacles.

### *NO POWER*

One reason for the pessimism about citizens is that they don't appear to have the power needed to have a significant impact on their communities, much less the country. Most haven't amassed huge amounts of money, large institutions are outside their control, and people don't have legal authority to act for the community. No wonder many citizens are seen—and see themselves—as politically powerless.

Unfortunately, the resources of citizens aren't always recognized, so they aren't put to use. One reason for this has to do with how power is understood. The resources of citizens give them little power *over* others but considerable power *with* them. That is evident in people's ability to gather and act through the variety of associations they create.

**THE RESOURCES OF CITIZENS GIVE THEM LITTLE POWER *OVER* OTHERS BUT CONSIDERABLE POWER *WITH* THEM. THAT IS EVIDENT IN PEOPLE'S ABILITY TO GATHER AND ACT THROUGH THE VARIETY OF ASSOCIATIONS THEY CREATE.**

One dramatic case I know of that shows these resources do actually exist, even if often unrecognized, comes from the work of John McKnight and his colleague Jody Kretzmann. Mentioned earlier, McKnight is one of the country's leading authorities on the untapped resources of communities, which he calls "assets." He and Kretzmann developed a novel approach to community organizing, called Asset-Based Community Development (ABCD), which has now inspired a global network. They disagreed with the conventional organizing strategy based on surveys of people's needs. In contrast, they began looking for unrecognized resources. Walking through neighborhoods in Chicago, the two asked people what they *could* do, rather than what they were lacking. The answers were often as simple as cooking, sewing, or fixing a car. Once recognized, however, these skills proved to be useful to local businesses.[48] The unemployed became employed. And the community benefited.

People can also combine their resources, making them more powerful. For example, those who could repair cars might join their individual skills and open a school on Saturdays to teach young people how to fix automobiles. Stories like those are more likely to exist where there are neighborhood associations that can identify resources and connect them. Not being bureaucratic, these grassroots groups can also respond quickly to problems by drawing on a wide range of talents and skills in neighborhoods.[49]

Although conventional wisdom holds that associations and other civic enterprises can't survive in places where people are consumed by day-to-day survival, Kretzmann and McKnight found more than 300 of these small, usually informal, groups in just one economically impoverished area.[50] (This number suggests that while some types of civic organizations are declining, new forms may be replacing them.)

**NOT BEING BUREAUCRATIC, THESE GRASSROOTS GROUPS CAN ALSO RESPOND QUICKLY TO PROBLEMS BY DRAWING ON A WIDE RANGE OF TALENTS AND SKILLS IN NEIGHBORHOODS.**

### *COLONIZATION*

Even though neighborhood and other grassroots associations are essential for citizens trying to make a difference in their communities, some have diminished their effectiveness, ironically, by being helped by larger organizations. Small associations are typically informal and lack much structure, so they have been called "Blobs." This term distinguishes them from formal organizations, which have been called "Squares," that have a staff, office, and legal charter. The two types of organizations serve different purposes and have different ways of doing what they do. The creator of TimeBanking, Edgar Cahn, picks up on the distinction between Blobs and Squares in his book, *No More Throw-Away People*, which is the basis for a very clever animation, "The Parable of the Blobs and Squares."[51]

Like Peter Block, Cahn recognizes that Blobs have energy and networks that can be useful in combating many community problems. Blobs are better at recognizing local resources and knowing how to use them. (Recall the story of Bruce Mundy.) Squares, on the other hand, know how to manage money and organize institutional action. They have resources like equipment and professional expertise. The Blobs have different kinds of resources, and some Squares recognize the value of those resources because they lack them. However, Cahn explains, "No matter how much the Squares . . . reach out in the community [to] get at the root causes of the problems," they seldom succeed; they can't mobilize the energy of a community.

This is why Squares want to partner with Blobs. The Squares try to help the Blobs by giving them money. Naturally, this means that the Blobs have to show financial accountability. Many Squares insist that the Blobs show measurable results from their projects. Grassroots groups, Cahn observes, "were taught to develop mission statements and strategic plans in order to remain 'true' to mission. Neighborhood leaders were trained in how to be Board members, how to conduct 'proper' meetings, [and] how to write and amend by-laws."[52] The unfortunate result was that these Blobs would lose the very qualities—like local credibility—that made them effective. Unintentionally, the Squares had "colonized" the Blobs, remaking them into little versions of themselves.

Although Cahn was describing nongovernmental Squares, what he observed can be just as true for government agencies. In order for any type of Square to work *with* Blobs, ways have to be found to minimize colonization. That requires recognizing the distinctive characteristics of Blobs. Blobs play essential roles in the ways they connect and engage people. What they do converts energy, even cynicism, into constructive action. They also promote norms that are essential to a democratic culture, norms like cooperation and mutual respect.

Human beings are social creatures and Blobs or informal associations are constantly forming, from neighborhood organizations to gangs. We ignore their importance—good and bad—at our peril.

### *INSTITUTIONAL BLIND SPOTS*

In her 2009 Nobel Prize-winning research, Elinor Ostrom shows that without the things citizens provide, few, if any, of our major institutions could do their jobs well. She called for institutions and their professionals to recognize citizens as "coproducers" in fields from education to public safety and social work.

Ostrom writes:

> If one presumes that teachers produce education, police produce safety, doctors and nurses produce health, and social workers produce effective households, the focus of attention is on how to professionalize the public service. Obviously, skilled teachers, police officers, medical personnel, and social workers are essential to the development of better public services. Ignoring the important role of children, families, support groups, neighborhood organizations, and churches

> in the production of these services means, however, that only a portion of the inputs to these processes are taken into account in the way that policy makers think about these problems. The term "client" is used more and more frequently to refer to those who should be viewed as essential co-producers of their own education, safety, health, and communities. A client is the name for a passive role. Being a co-producer makes one an active partner.[53]

The obstacle to coproduction is that what citizens have to offer isn't recognized or is too difficult to integrate into the work of institutions. Still, products from the work of citizens can complement what institutions do because, as I've said, the work of citizens is different from the work of institutions. (Recall the discussion in chapter 1.) I am not talking about people volunteering to help teachers and health-care professionals. Although very commendable, this kind of volunteering is doing the work of the institutions. I'm talking about citizens doing their own, distinctive work. When that happens, citizens become not just *coproducers*, but *complementary producers*. As I hope was clear in the cases presented in chapter 1, I have in mind supplementary projects in health care, education, and other areas where people do things professionals don't—and can't—do. Because of this difference, I like the term *complementary production* rather than *coproduction*.

This book began by saying that "better and stronger" meant democratic. The complementary production of public goods by citizens is significant democratically because people are making a difference. An additional benefit of complementary production is that it can improve the relationship between the citizenry and the institutions created to serve the public (governments, schools, etc.). This is the relationship that is often troubled by a lack of public confidence. And that is often because people feel they can't influence the institutions. However, people who say they have a good relationship with institutions such as schools may add, "And I am involved with it," meaning they are contributing something meaningful.[54]

## UNINFORMED

The perception that regular citizens don't know enough to govern themselves has increased, even as the amount of available information has grown to mind-boggling levels. A report in the *Economist* describes citizens as helpless amateurs in a world run on professional expertise.[55] The situation as such is the obituary for a democratic citizenry because it replaces the people (the *demos* in *democracy*) as the sovereign power (the *kratos* in *democracy*). Is there any counter to this argument, and is it recognized? The answer is mixed—"yes" to the first part and "maybe" to the second.

**COLLECTIVE INTELLIGENCE:** The counter to writing off citizens is in the prehistory of our species. Human beings have survived millions of years of dangers and calamities (some of their own making) by relying on their collective intelligence. That intelligence is developed by combining different experiences into a more comprehensive and shared understanding of the realities that people face. Collective intelligence allows people to recognize the goods they hold in common; that is, to recognize what is valuable for their collective well-being. This is shared knowledge.[56]

Shared knowledge comes from communities. An "awareness that knowledge lives in a community," Steven Sloman and Phillip Fernbach wrote in *The Knowledge Illusion*, "gives us a different way to conceive of intelligence." They mean "different" as compared to the conventional definition of intelligence that is based on personal IQ. A more pertinent concept of intelligence, they argue, is the ability to contribute to a group's or a community's way of thinking. The most valuable knowledge for survival is knowing how to work together.[57] A community with that kind of intelligence is more than a place with smart individuals; it is a smart community.[58]

### POOR JUDGMENT

The greatest challenge to the claim that regular people can make a difference in our political systems—that we can rule ourselves—is that whatever information or knowledge we have, we are notorious for making bad decisions. It has been argued that we aren't even good judges of what is best for us. We are subject to prejudices and other biases. All of that is true, yet it isn't the whole story.

My objective here isn't to go into the complexities of human intelligence, but to shift to what is known about using our brains to make good collective decisions. Over the eons of our existence, humans have become "programmed" to make decisions about what to do when there is more than one option to consider and no accepted authority to say which is best.[59] These situations lead to questions about what *should* be done. They are normative. And there are no experts on such matters. We have to rely on our best judgment when making these decisions. Our faculty for judgment is implicated in many ancient languages, which have words for collective decision-making. In English, the word for exercising the faculty for good judgment is *deliberation*. It comes from Latin and means "to weigh carefully" as on a balance scale.

**DELIBERATING TOGETHER TO ACT TOGETHER:** Public deliberation exercises our faculty for making sound, collective judgments about what collective actions to take. But like any exercise, we have to do it repeatedly.

**PUBLIC DELIBERATION EXERCISES OUR FACULTY FOR MAKING SOUND, COLLECTIVE JUDGMENTS ABOUT WHAT COLLECTIVE ACTIONS TO TAKE. BUT LIKE ANY EXERCISE, WE HAVE TO DO IT REPEATEDLY.**

There is no such thing as infallible decision-making. We consider a judgment sound when it is consistent with what is considered most valuable in a particular situation.

At the deepest level, all humans want security from danger, freedom to act as they think best, fair treatment, and some control over their future. These are survival imperatives. Yet in different circumstances, these imperatives pull us in different directions. Deciding what we should do requires the exercise of judgment through deliberation.

Even though humans aren't infallible, deliberations over time improve the chances that our decisions will be sound. However, just because we have a faculty for judgment doesn't mean we always use it. (I certainly don't.) Collective or public decision-making is difficult, and there are thousands of ways to avoid it, especially in a political culture that promotes sound-bites and partisan attacks.

Deliberation begins in deciding what the issue facing us is in terms of what we consider valuable. Then the decision-making moves toward laying out the possible options for dealing with the problem. The shorthand terms for the initial phases in deliberation are "naming" problems and "framing" options for action. The naming is important because the wrong diagnosis can be fatal. Framing options is also crucial because if the options are just about whom to blame for the problem, it almost guarantees that the community won't be able to come together to effectively combat the dangers facing them.

**DELIBERATION IN PRACTICE:** The most convincing evidence I know of that people have a faculty for shared judgment comes from decades of observing nonpartisan National Issues Forums (NIF), which are intended to be deliberative, and not just civil, informed discussions. The Kettering Foundation doesn't hold forums, but it does use its research to prepare briefing materials that have been used in forums organized by thousands of local civic organizations, religious institutions, schools, colleges, libraries—even prisons. NIF's Common Ground for Action brought deliberation online. And in 2020, all deliberations moved online, including on Zoom.[60]

NIF briefing books, or issue guides, have covered most major issues, including contentious ones like immigration, abortion, and freedom of speech. These issue briefs give people at least three options for actions to consider. The briefs point out the pros and cons of each option, emphasizing the tensions among the many things people consider deeply valuable. (For example, increasing security measures may also restrict freedom.) These materials encourage giving each option, even the unpopular ones, a "fair trial." And recognizing the tensions has led to exercising people's faculty for judgment.

Forum sponsors have seldom found the meetings to be acrimonious, although participants have spoken candidly and with strong feelings. Everyone coming to these forums expects to hear different opinions. I recall the story of a forum in Texas that included those who favored the open possession of guns. Even though "open carry" wasn't endorsed by most forum participants, they wanted to know why its advocates had come to support it. Hearing stories of the experiences of the advocates helped provide a broader, more comprehensive understanding of the issue. And this willingness changed the tone of the decision-making. At the end of the meeting, the "open carry" group was interested in holding more forums.[61]

**A PIVOT:** Participants in other deliberative forums also report that communities benefit from a change in the tone of political conversations, which they call a "pivot" toward greater listening. For example, in a forum using an NIF briefing book on AIDS, one participant, sincerely convinced that the disease was God's punishment for the wicked, sat in the front row, ready to deliver his message. (He had disrupted previous discussions on the issue.) In this forum, he was asked to speak first, and he restated his unequivocal opinion. But then someone else asked whether there were any others who thought the AIDS issue had a moral dimension. Nearly everyone raised a hand. That response drew the first speaker into the group rather than pushing him out. He saw that he wasn't the only one who valued moral order. While his point of view didn't change significantly and few shared it, the way he participated did. He lowered his voice; he seemed to listen more. The tenor of the meeting changed despite the differences in opinion, and that helped the community to move forward in responding to the AIDS crisis.

**DISCOVERING THE AREA BETWEEN AGREEMENT AND DISAGREEMENT:** Deliberative forums don't force everyone to agree, but they do help communities move forward when full agreement isn't possible. The forums do that by locating the area between agreement and disagreement. That is the practical arena where people don't fully agree but can find things to do that they can live with—for a while. I would also include as deliberative the community forums patterned after the NIF briefing books. Recall the breast cancer forums that Dr. Hullett organized, which were described in chapter 1.

Although we hold many of the same things dear, we differ on priorities. And that is what causes tensions. However, human beings are naturally curious and many forums report that people often want to hear about these differences, without changing their positions. "I still think you are wrong, but I can understand why you think as you do." No one says that exactly, but this prompts some people to really listen to others. And what they take in by listening allows them to learn even from those they oppose. That is how they get a more complete sense of the complexities in the issues.

This learning, or discovering, is crucial in order for communities to broaden civic engagement and combat serious problems. This is the learning together that I mentioned earlier. Of course, openness to others isn't likely to occur when issues are framed in adversarial terms and people are fearful of being attacked. That is why a deliberative framing of issues is so important.

**OPENNESS TO OTHERS ISN'T LIKELY TO OCCUR WHEN ISSUES ARE FRAMED IN ADVERSARIAL TERMS AND PEOPLE ARE FEARFUL OF BEING ATTACKED. THAT IS WHY A DELIBERATIVE FRAMING OF ISSUES IS SO IMPORTANT.**

### *TOO DIVIDED!*

Another challenge to engaging the citizenry is that the public is too divided to have anything coherent to offer. "Talking to the public is a waste of time; you can hear anything." That is often the reaction to a public engagement initiative. So the foundation decided to look at what effect, if any, deliberations had on divisiveness. Studies show that simple discussions can actually intensify disagreement.[62] Deliberation is no cure-all, but it does have something to offer in a contentious environment. I have already mentioned the ability to change the tenor of conversations on contentious issues.

People do tend to pay attention to arguments they like and disregard what they don't. However, deliberative decision-making takes people into the practical side of politics, which is less ideological. For instance, the issue in one case was how to deal with a drainage system that leaked sewage into people's homes. Before that happened, people had been divided on religious grounds. However, sewage isn't a theological issue. When focusing on such practical problems, deliberation doesn't eliminate differences but offers communities a more constructive way to deal with them.

## *ONLY A FEW*

One of the most common obstacles to recognizing the benefits of deliberation is the perception that it can be done only by well-educated people. Participants in forums sponsored by academic institutions are often well educated. That being recognized, there have been no reports of any groups who lacked the capacity for making sound decisions. Professor Bonnie Braun and a research team at the University of Maryland studied deliberative forums involving women from poor, rural communities. Their research did not show any lack of capacity for deliberating.[63]

Public deliberation isn't one of the many facilitated group processes. It isn't a special technique to be learned (although practice helps). As has been said, deliberating is just the exercise of our natural faculty for judgment. The purpose of the forums isn't to get deliberation "up to scale." The ability to deliberate is already up to scale. The objective of the forums is to give practical demonstrations so that deliberation will be used more often wherever community decisions are made.

Deliberation also counters divisiveness in the way problems are named to capture the basic things all humans hold dear, like safety from danger. The recognition that many of our disagreements have to do with different circumstances and experiences helps turn the decision-making from people versus people to people versus problems.

The obstacles to citizens making a significant difference are formidable though not necessarily overwhelming. There are ways for citizens and their communities to overcome them. Encourage but don't colonize Blobs. Foster deliberation wherever public decisions are made. The list goes on.

## WHAT'S NEXT?

All the problems that citizens and communities face aren't the same. Where I live, my lane, which joins the street to town, has a deep pothole. It jolts my car. We've called the appropriate municipal department. They will repair it, before winter weather sets in, I hope. This is an aggravating problem, but it isn't a deep-seated one. You might say it's relatively "tame" as problems go. Other problems aren't so obvious and have no quick fix.

The introduction makes a passing reference to the "wickedness" in some problems. This isn't just a dramatic flourish. There is research that distinguishes between relatively tame and wicked problems.[64] The case is made that the country solved major but "tame" problems by using improved technology and professional expertise. We built a national highway system that linked east to west and north to south. We developed a banking system that protects against the causes of the Great Depression.

But those achievements didn't eliminate the need to deal with problems that technology and scientific expertise alone can't solve. These are problems where the question is, What *should* be done? A strategy for responding to them is the subject of chapter 3.

CHAPTER THREE

# A STRATEGY FOR DEALING WITH THE WICKEDNESS IN PROBLEMS

Earlier, I said that the typical way of solving most community problems is based on a successful strategy that was developed in the wake of the disastrously destructive Great Depression. This strategy helped the United States make many useful improvements. Some problems, however, proved immune to the standard remedy. Their characteristics have been described as "wicked."

To combat these problems, a community-as-a-whole has to respond because the difficulties have many sources, which come from different parts of a community. That requires a level of civic engagement that goes beyond the involvement of local leaders, however able they may be. Of course, it's unlikely that everyone in an entire community will respond. So, I've used the phrase "community-as-a-whole" to describe when every sector of the community is engaged in attacking a problem. If the causes come from everywhere, so must the responses.

## COMMUNITY POLITICS AS USUAL

The usual strategy for solving problems is familiar. When a community faces a difficulty, local officials and leading citizens follow a set pattern. They often turn to experts to diagnose the problem. Then they cut the problem down to a manageable size. To act quickly, they decide on a solution and develop a plan to implement it as efficiently as possible. If there is a model to follow or best practices to emulate, all the better. A lead institution may be designated to carry out the plan, which usually includes selling the public on what the leadership believes is best. Goals are set with metrics for determining success and holding the responsible parties accountable.

### *UNINTENDED CONSEQUENCES*

Despite the merits of the usual way of responding to community problems—and there are many—the results may not be what was intended; in fact, they may be quite counterproductive.

**FRAGMENTATION:** When we define a problem to make it manageable, we may unwittingly fragment it. Breaking complex problems apart can lead to overlooking vital interconnections. Consider what can happen when we try to help young people who wind up on the margins of society. There are as many organizations providing services as there are labels for what afflicts youngsters. Typically, young people are categorized according to the particular difficulties they are experiencing. Then they are assigned to agencies whose missions correspond to the labels the youngsters have been given. Dropouts may be sent to special schools. Disruptive students are put with teachers or counselors who are trained to deal with them. Teenage mothers-to-be are assisted by federal nutrition programs. Children with emotional problems may be seen by community social service organizations. Although each of these agencies benefits the young people, the left hand may not know what the right hand is doing. Even though the categories of risk are logical, they ignore an important reality: youngsters are whole people whose maladies are interrelated.

**SOLUTION WARS:** Pressure to find the "right solution" can send a community into a never-ending battle between proponents of different plans. Those who rush to a solution might say that everybody already knows what the problem is. Actually, what people "know" may be only their own understanding of a problem. Communities have spent considerable energy debating which of a number of predetermined solutions is best, not recognizing that there is no agreement on the nature of the problem. How a problem is understood varies with people's circumstances and experiences. Unless these differences are recognized in the way a problem is described, or "named," people aren't likely to work together as a community.

**PERVERSIONS OF ACCOUNTABILITY:** When management of a project is transferred to an institution, citizens often try to maintain control by insisting on strict accountability. This, too, can produce unintended consequences.

Suppose a school board wants to respond to the public by making changes people want. The board makes a new policy or issues a directive mandating that the school system and the superintendent act in certain ways. Operating through a bureaucracy, the superintendent translates the mandate into measurable objectives and appropriate procedures for principals. Principals then pass these along to teachers, usually with the requirement that they fill out forms to show that they have followed the mandated procedures.

The requirement to have measurable results is understandable (to ensure accountability), yet that can be a prime source for unintended consequences. The desired results are not always quantifiable As survey research scholar Dan Yankelovich has said:

> The first step is to measure whatever can be easily measured. That is OK as far as it goes. The second step is to disregard that which can't be measured or give it an arbitrary quantitative value. This is artificial and misleading. The third step is to presume that what can't be easily measured really isn't very important. This is blindness. The fourth step is to say that what can't be easily measured doesn't exist. This is suicide.[65]

Demonstrating accountability—the intended result—isn't achieved because of an overreliance on quantitative measures or because citizens differ with institutional leaders over what are valid indications of accountability. There are also differences over the meaning of accountability itself. Although institutional leaders typically have in mind information as evidence of results, citizens look for accountability in the nature of the relationship they have with governmental and nongovernmental institutions, including schools.[66] When accountability is institutionally defined, it tends to disenfranchise citizens. People want, instead, a relationship that is open, accessible, and based on shared concerns. They want to know whether the institutions care about what *they* care about. If so, then people might be more likely to work together with schools.

Many Americans have not only been critical of the schools, they have had a declining sense of ownership and responsibility. People may not think that *the* schools are really *their* schools, even though the schools are funded by their tax dollars. Ideally, citizens should feel that they, and their communities, not just the schools, are accountable for what happens to the next generation. Or, at a minimum, citizens should decide who is accountable—and for what.[67]

Often citizens and institutional leaders talk past one another when it comes to being accountable. School officials may think that their institutions are models of accountability, citing the voluminous test score data they publish. They believe these performance measures are in line with the public's demand for higher standards. Citizens, however,

while appreciating the information on test performance, may still not be persuaded that the schools are doing the job they expect them to do. Although most people want students held to high expectations, they may also think that test scores are only one indication of school performance.[68] And while the educators' intentions are commendable, each step in institutionally defined accountability tends to compromise the responsiveness that many people are looking for. Furthermore, the interactions between officials and those being served diminishes. In the case of schools, the community reinforcement that students and educators need declines.

**ALTHOUGH MOST PEOPLE WANT STUDENTS HELD TO HIGH EXPECTATIONS, THEY MAY ALSO THINK THAT TEST SCORES ARE ONLY ONE INDICATION OF SCHOOL PERFORMANCE.**

### *DELEGATING UNDELEGABLE RESPONSIBILITY*

Accountability has to be shared. Education can't be just the responsibility of the schools. Health can't be left just to the medical system. Crime can't be the sole responsibility of law enforcement. Doing so would overlook what citizens must do, as Elinor Ostrom shows in her research on coproduction.[69]

Institutions become overburdened without support from citizens and communities and the things that only they can provide. As reported in chapter 1, the importance of citizens and their communities is evident in everything from health and education to social welfare and economic development. Yet the usual strategy for addressing community problems doesn't typically take into account the work that needs to be done by the public. The citizenry has some undelegable responsibilities.

### *APPROVING ISN'T OWNING*

Even when citizens participate in reviewing the leadership's plan or have had a voice in constructing a budget, they may not have the sense of ownership and responsibility that is needed in order for them to do the coproducing. If people don't actually produce anything by their own work, they aren't likely to feel full ownership. Human beings take more responsibility for what they have made themselves than for what has been made for them. A persuaded public, even if it accepts a plan, isn't likely to generate much political will to implement it.

## THE CHALLENGES OF WICKEDNESS

Despite some unintended consequences, conventional strategies are usually effective in dealing with conventional problems. However, all problems aren't the conventional kind. Some have wicked characteristics. I have already mentioned some of these but more needs to be said. Because the very nature of these problems is unclear, the diagnosis or name is problematic. There is no shared understanding of what is troubling the community. Each symptom is related to another in a never-ending chain. These problems are as tricky as they are aggressive. Furthermore, they are persistent; they never go away completely because they are embedded in the community.[70]

No one institution or profession can eliminate problems with these characteristics. There must be multifaceted responses, which have to be mutually supportive. Centralized, bureaucratic coordination isn't likely to be effective; for one reason, it's costly and cumbersome. Most difficult of all, any effective action has to close a yawning gap between what is happening and what people think *should* be happening. Yet there is no agreement about what ought to be done to close the gap.

## ANOTHER STRATEGY?

For the reasons I've just cited, I think the wickedness in problems calls for more than the usual problem-solving strategy. The typical strategy doesn't match up well with the challenges that wickedness presents. For example, because the nature of wicked problems is in doubt or contested, an effective strategy has to pay more attention to how the problem is named. Citizens are prone to describe a problem in terms of how it affects their lives and the things they care about. They don't see problems through the lenses that experts use; they see problems in the ways they experience them. Furthermore, given that there are no technical solutions, the responses have to go beyond those that experts provide. And because there are multiple causes, sources, and locations, citizens and organizations in every part of the community have to be engaged. Also, no one institution can meet all the demands, and those that are called on must have supportive, complementary work coming from the citizenry of a community. And decision-making about what should be done to counter a wicked problem has to contend with multiple, often conflicting, opinions about what *should* happen. This decision-making requires the deliberation that exercises people's faculty for judgment. Finally, because wicked problems are persistent, communities have to keep up their problem-solving engagement. They can't declare victory and go home.

## LEARNING TOGETHER TO WORK TOGETHER

As I was rereading this next section, I was struck by how puzzling this heading may sound. People's first impression is likely to be that I am talking about classroom instruction or an online course. I'm not. I am talking about a kind of learning that stimulates new perspectives on old problems and results in discoveries of better ways to respond to wicked challenges.

The goal of the learning strategy I have in mind is to encourage people who are not alike, and who may not even like one another, to work together because they recognize they need one another. In other words, the objective is for people with different perspectives and concerns to better understand one another, even if they never completely agree.

### *DEALING WITH DIFFERENCES IN PERCEPTIONS AND CONCERNS*

People who volunteer to take on a leadership role are essential to a community's well-being. I often cite my cousin, Marion Bumpers (Bumpy), who, in her 90s, continued to rally others in my hometown to do everything from organizing bus excursions for seniors to baking goods to sell at the historical society's events.

Community leaders like Bumpy, however, are often frustrated by the lack of participation by their fellow citizens. Community leaders worry that the civic muscles needed to make democracy work will grow weaker from lack of use. If there is an obvious emergency like a tornado, most people get off their supposed "couches" and respond. Yet after the crisis passes, life returns to the usual routines. That might be fine if it weren't for the wickedness in problems accumulating and eating away at the capacity of a community to respond when the next disaster strikes.

The supposedly apathetic tell a different story. They care about their families, their health, their jobs, and their personal finances. The concept of "community" may strike them as too abstract. They will talk to you about a troublesome neighbor or their impatience with the bureaucracies they encounter or their frustrations at work. These people aren't apathetic; they just don't care about the things that the leaders want them to care about. And, most significant, as I've said, they are reluctant to get involved because they doubt they can make any difference combating the problems they do care about.

**DIFFERENCES IN PERSPECTIVES BETWEEN THOSE IN LEADERSHIP ROLES AND REGULAR CITIZENS AREN'T SO BLATANT AND DIVISIVE THAT THEY MAKE THE NEWS. THE DIFFERENCES ARE "JUST THE WAY THINGS ARE."**

The differences in perspectives between those in leadership roles and regular citizens aren't so blatant and divisive that they make the news. The differences are "just the way things are." These two groups talk and rub shoulders every day. However, they may have different points of view. And they may have very different perceptions of what is or isn't happening in the place where they live.

### LEARNING TOGETHER

The challenge isn't to eliminate these differences in perceptions. That's impossible. It is to keep them from interfering with the community-wide engagement required in the continuing battle with wickedness. Even though differences among citizens will always exist in diverse communities, it may be possible for a community to give people other experiences that they can share, experiences that connect, not eliminate, differences in perspectives and concerns. The experience of others is a transforming force for the learning together that I'm talking about.

**CONNECTING DIFFERENCES:** Throughout human history, learning together has been key to survival. The earliest human ancestors weren't bigger or stronger than their competitors. Yet they grew from a small group in one corner of the world to a population that now spans the globe. How did that happen? One major reason was their ability to learn from one another and to pass on the lessons learned to new generations. This learning comes from combining different perspectives to gain a better, more comprehensive and shared understanding of what is happening to us and around us.

**LEVELING THE PLAYING FIELD:** Because learning together benefits from diverse experience, it creates a certain equality among people, which is critical in responding to problems that require action throughout a community. The ability to contribute to the group or community is more important than the other considerations that usually determine an individual's status. Economic or social advantages don't count as much as adding to a community's learning. This learning enables people with different perspectives and concerns to get, if not on the same page, at least on related pages. That is essential when the perspectives and concerns of people in leadership roles is different from those of other people.

**LEARNING TO DISCOVER:** The learning that involves acquiring information or developing a skill is linked to individual intelligence, or IQ. However, the learning I have been talking about draws on what I called earlier "collective intelligence." We use it to make discoveries about ourselves, our fellow citizens, and our communities. These discoveries occur when people are engaged with one another in ways that facilitate new insights into solving problems. A truly smart community is one that has developed the ability to learn from itself about itself.

One of the most important discoveries is that people consider many of the same things, such as being treated fairly, deeply valuable. We draw on what is most valuable in making decisions about what should be done in our communities. Also, the things held dear engage us; they are our self-starters. We don't have to be persuaded by someone else to become involved.

**THE CATALYSTS, ANOTHER PERSPECTIVE:** Philosopher Merab Mamardashvili explained how taking into consideration other people's experiences creates a new vantage point for understanding problems. Problems with wicked characteristics can't be understood if seen only from the vantage point afforded by the usual strategies for problem solving. As an illustration, Mamardashvili built on a story by Albert Einstein. Here is my version of his version of Einstein's story. (I hope you are impressed by the reference to Einstein.)

**THESE DISCOVERIES OCCUR WHEN PEOPLE ARE ENGAGED WITH ONE ANOTHER IN WAYS THAT FACILITATE NEW INSIGHTS INTO SOLVING PROBLEMS.**

Imagine a little bug, a beetle, crawling on a large white ball, perhaps a billiard ball. Everywhere this beetle goes—forward, backward, to the right, to the left—it sees nothing but white space. Now, imagine that a philosopher appears and asks the beetle, "Is space finite or infinite?" Based on its own experience, the bug says, quickly and assuredly, "Space is infinite. Everywhere I go every day, it is the same. I see an endless white surface." Then the philosopher picks the bug up off the ball and holds it high. The philosopher asks again, "Is space finite or infinite?" Now, the bug realizes that its space is not infinite at all. It is very finite. The point of the story is that other experiences, like the philosopher giving the beetle a new vantage point, provide us a different understanding of reality—the reality of our "ball," our community.[71]

In community learning, the experiences of others can do what the philosopher did—provide another perspective. Sharing experiences with different people can alter the understanding of a problem and reveal how it might be combated more effectively. A learning strategy is built around this exchange of perspectives.

As I mentioned in chapter 2, deliberation can open the door to considering different experiences when issues are not presented or framed in adversarial ways, even though they *are* framed to show the tensions among the things people hold dear. An effective framing shifts the focus of the decision-making from whom to blame to the different pulls and tugs of all that we ourselves hold valuable. Deliberating is working through these tensions to the point where communities can move forward, but it is also a way of learning.

### *GENERATING POLITICAL WILL*

Dealing effectively with wickedness, however, requires more than recognizing differences in experiences and working through conflicting opinions. Combating the persistence in problems also requires sustained political will and energy. Learning together is a source of that energy. When people make discoveries by deliberating, it generates political will. These discoveries are insights that show attractive possibilities for improvements. Seeing these possibilities helps keep up the civic momentum needed when faced with persistent problems. People are motivated by discoveries of how better to approach old problems. Communities that are continually learning are also less likely to stop when they fail. Their learning helps them profit from mistakes.

## LEARNING EXCHANGES

To be effective, learning together has to have places set aside to encourage it. A leadership or community development program, for example, can create a learning exchange. These exchanges can also occur when worried citizens meet regularly in informal groups.

In a small West Virginia town of about 5,000, a group of concerned citizens met for lunch every week to talk about economic development. Once a center of commerce, the town had lost businesses, which were not likely to return. The subject at the lunches was how the community could create a resilient economy. The assumption was that citizens themselves would have to be active in rebuilding the economy. They didn't think they could wait on attracting businesses from some other county or community. That realization prompted the group to start inventorying what they could do to make their town a better place to live and work.[72] This was an informal exchange for learning together, yet it had some of the elements of the more formal exchanges that take place in educational and civic organizations.

Wherever exchanges are located, participants have to move beyond talking among themselves and engage the community-as-a-whole in the work that citizens need to do. When that happens, the people in the learning exchanges are likely to realize that citizens working together to strengthen their community, in and of itself, begins to make the community a better place.

## *CONVENING AND NETWORKING*

I'm not sure that the West Virginia "club" had a president. Whoever sponsors, hosts, or convenes meetings of this sort can't be at the center of the discussions. Still, the convenor has important roles to play. The main one is that of a catalyst, offering suggestions to consider and encouraging others to share theirs. Looking for opportunities to connect initiatives, convenors also provide essential structure with a minimum of control. They understand the importance of what they *don't* do. By minimizing their control, they create opportunities for others to act.[73]

The best example I have of the role convenors should play comes from the Highlander Research and Education Center. One of the school's founders, Myles Horton, recalled the time a union strike committee came to Highlander for guidance. Facing powerful opposition, the strikers were desperate and insisted Horton tell them what to do. Horton refused, even when one of the strikers threatened to shoot him, saying, in effect, "You are the expert; you know the answers; give them to us!" Horton responded, "In the first place, I don't know what to do, and if I did know what to do I wouldn't tell you because if I had to tell you today then I'd have to tell you tomorrow, and when I'm gone you'd have to get somebody else to tell you." Horton confessed that when he heard the threat, he was tempted to become an instant expert. Instead, he told the man with the pistol, "No. Go ahead and shoot if you want to, but I'm not going to tell you." Fortunately, the other strikers calmed the gunman down. Horton's response shows the importance of people learning to make decisions for themselves. Convenors of learning exchanges have to avoid being experts with answers and, instead, become promoters of shared learning—hopefully without facing a gun.[74]

Convenors can also encourage networking among exchange participants. This helps people to stay connected and collaborate. Networks allow information to circulate freely and quickly because there isn't a central hub that everyone has to go through. The relationships among the participants and the expectations they have of one another in networking are especially important. Networks aren't command structures with rules to follow.

Even if a learning exchange lasts for a year or more, it won't be enough to change the way a community goes about solving problems. So rather than trying to get up to scale, an exchange might try encouraging other exchanges in different parts of the community. When that happens, learning together is more likely to develop into a community-wide or even a statewide network of exchanges. (Chapter 6 will take up this challenge.)

Exchanges for learning together are based on two requirements that appear contradictory at first glance, yet aren't. Self-responsibility for learning in an exchange goes hand in hand with what may appear to be the opposite, which is shared or joint responsibility for the exchange itself. The wagon trains that pioneers used to travel to the frontier provide a rough analogy. (I watched a lot of Westerns when I was a boy, so I know what happened.) Each family was responsible for its own wagon, yet they all had to cooperate to protect the train. When robbers threatened to attack (which happened every Saturday in the movies), the pioneers circled their wagons for joint defense. The same is true in shared learning; the participants are all in it together. It is a relationship among self-responsible parties who take ownership of their own learning. In the exchanges, the people involved learn with and *from* others. But no one can learn *for* someone else.

## EXPERIMENTATION AND RESILIENCE

Learning in order to discover requires tapping into people's curiosity. That leads to experimenting with different approaches to a problem, some of which will inevitably fail. A community bent on success may have difficulty with experiments that are "trial and error." One of the values of a learning strategy is building an appreciation for trying new approaches to old problems.

**ONE OF THE VALUES OF A LEARNING STRATEGY IS BUILDING AN APPRECIATION FOR TRYING NEW APPROACHES TO OLD PROBLEMS.**

Experimentation, however, has "costs" that may not be acceptable when a community is desperate to solve a pressing problem. These costs include the uncertainty experimentation brings with it, along with the lack of quick, tangible results and popular acclaim that comes from "success." A learning culture provides the capital to offset these costs. If a great many people are involved in conducting experiments, it makes trying new approaches the norm rather than the rare exception.

A culture that appreciates learning and continuous improvement rather than dramatic success can have very practical results. Communities that aim for immediate success tend to stop working when their project goals have been met. This can occur even if problems remain. On the other hand, communities with projects that don't succeed are disappointed, and they, too, stop. So, success and failure can have the same result: communities quit. The wickedness in problems, however, is persistent.

Learning communities should be able to keep pushing ahead because they look beyond short-term results and failures. These communities are more resilient. They appreciate the sentiment of the writer Rudyard Kipling, who called success or failure "imposters" to be treated "just the same."[75]

A community that has multiple learning exchanges connected through networks strengthens the civic culture. When that happens, collective learning is more likely to be used in the regular business of a community. This learning enables a community to be resilient when there are setbacks. And gains made in a crisis are less likely to be lost because of the importance attached to continuing to learn together as a stimulus to working together.

## WHAT'S NEXT?

The story line in this chapter sets the stage for the next two chapters. This chapter addressed the challenge of wickedness, which the usual approach to community problem-solving isn't suited to combat. A community learning strategy is suggested here, not as a replacement for, but as an addition to, other strategies. This strategy takes up two difficulties that were described in the first chapters: community leaders' frustrations with the lack of public engagement and citizens' doubts about their ability to make a significant difference in the political system. Learning together is a way of connecting people with such different perceptions and frustrations. And it is a way for people to discover their innate abilities and resources, such as the ability to deliberate in making the decision to work together, which is key to acting together.

This chapter ends with an account of how learning to discover works, which is by using the diversity of experiences in a community to get a broad, integrated understanding of the community. This improved or enlarged understanding can reveal new possibilities for combating problems.

Having made learning central, this book needs to move into a learning mode itself. The first three chapters provide information about communities taken from research. Now, the community where the readers live has to generate its own information. So, chapters 4 and 5 will propose types of questions to be used for a community checkup that might provide a new shared perspective on familiar local terrain. These are simple questions like Merab Mamardashvili's. Readers may want to adapt them to fit their particular communities.

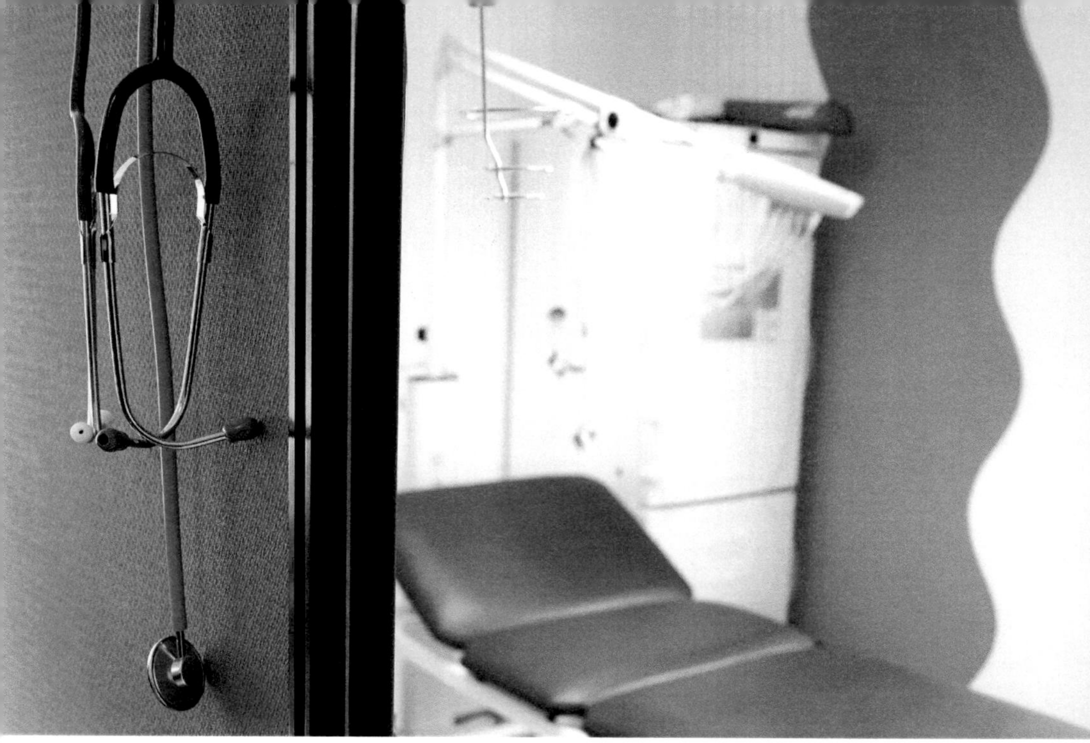

CHAPTER FOUR

# A COMMUNITY CHECKUP

To review a bit: Communities are key to everything from the health of their people to the education of children to long-term economic prosperity. Many of the things communities do must be done by citizens working together. In fact, some of these things can be done only by citizens, who have to be producers in a strong democracy, not just consumers. Of course, there have always been doubts about the competence of citizens, and these doubts can't be tossed aside. However, citizens have resources they can use and innate abilities they can draw on. The things citizens can do are especially important in combating the wickedness in some problems, which requires people to be constantly learning, especially from their failures, so they can discover new ways to combat old difficulties. Learning and discovering together helps keep up the engagement of the community-as-a-whole, which is essential in combating these persistent problems.

This chapter is designed for people to gather their own information about their own community. It includes some questions you might want to consider when doing a community checkup. A checkup can kick off learning together. The areas that you might look at more closely are areas characteristic of high-achieving communities. These are not perfect communities, yet they do better at solving their problems than communities with greater advantages. Under stress, high-achieving communities are resilient. They are more likely to come together than fall apart. (For research on resilience, I suggest Vaughn Grisham Jr.'s multiyear study of Tupelo, Mississippi.)[76]

## LEADERS OR LEADERFUL?

One characteristic of high-achieving communities has to do with leadership. Something you and the others reading this book might want to look at more closely is the leadership in your community. High achievers have many people from different neighborhoods or areas in the town who take some initiative to solve problems. However, these communities don't necessarily have the best leaders—*best* meaning "renowned or influential." Don't misunderstand me; it is great to have people like that. Still, high achievers call upon numerous leaders or initiative takers that come from all parts of the community.

These communities are "leaderful."[77] And this makes it possible to deal with wicked problems that have sources in many locations dispersed throughout a community.

You might look at how leaderful your community is. In addition to leaders in positions of authority (the mayor, council members, president of the chamber of commerce), who is taking the initiative in responding to problems? What sections of town do these initiators call home? That is, how dispersed are they? Does where they live match the locations of the sources of the problems?

When describing what their community needs most, people will often say "good leaders." They are right. But good leaders can come, and must come, from throughout a community. The more, the better because they will encourage others to take needed initiative. Furthermore, the most effective leaders won't be gatekeepers in control; they will be door openers who are skilled at building community networks. You might check up on "door openers" and network builders, and where they can be found.

**GOOD LEADERS CAN COME, AND MUST COME, FROM THROUGHOUT A COMMUNITY. THE MORE, THE BETTER.**

A study by Rich Harwood compared a community that was adept at problem solving with a similar community that wasn't.[78] The study showed that the town that wasn't doing so well actually had "better" leaders, as traditionally understood. These leaders were highly educated, personally successful, and civically responsible. Yet what stood out in the problem-solving community wasn't so much the qualifications of the leaders as their number. And they were from different parts of the community. Most significant of all was the way they interacted with other citizens; they were, indeed, more like door openers than gatekeepers. This community was leaderful. It had 10 times more people providing leadership than the community with the "best" leaders. Because of that, the leaderful community had a stronger democracy. As Woodrow Wilson once said, "I believe in democracy because it releases the energies of every human being.[79]

And Henrik Ibsen reminds us that "a community is like a ship; everyone ought to be prepared to take the helm."[80] Given the difficulties every community faces, from drug abuse to the breakdown of families, a few good leaders won't be enough. Leadership and citizenship need to become synonymous. Resilient communities make leadership everybody's business, not just the business of a few. They don't equate leadership exclusively with positions of authority.[81] These are some of the reasons you might want to check up on your community's leadership.[82]

## CITIZENS: CONSUMERS OR PRODUCERS?

There is no more important place to look for civic strength in a community than within the people who live there. How do people see their role as citizens? Do they think of themselves as simply residents who just obey laws, pay taxes, and maybe vote? Does their understanding of citizenship go beyond that? Do people think of themselves as actors, not merely objects of the actions of others? The stronger a community is, the more likely there are people who see they have a role in the production of tangible and intangible "goods" that make the place they live better for everyone. These "goods" can be as simple as a community-built playground to provide a safe place for neighborhood children. This sense of being a producer gives citizens a feeling of ownership, which leads to taking responsibility for their community.

How people see themselves is also influenced by how others see them. You might want to look at the way local institutions are organized to treat citizens. For hospitals, are they just patients? For businesses, are they just customers? For law firms, are they just clients? For the news media, are they simply readers and viewers? For educational institutions, are students treated as actors? In the civics classes taught in the schools, how are citizens portrayed?

## ASSOCIATIONS

Another place to look during a checkup is for the small, informal, grassroots associations or Blobs. The number and location of these civic groups is a good indication of the number of opportunities there are for people to work together, which enables them to make a difference. Blobs may not be easy to find because many don't have street addresses. Yet recall that McKnight and Kretzmann found hundreds of these groups in one of the poorer sections of Chicago.[83] Are they turning frustration, anger, and negative energy into positive energy? Have they avoided becoming bureaucratic Squares? Do they respond quickly when there is a crisis? Grassroots associations themselves are a resource. Do they know where to find more resources, particularly untapped ones?[84]

Also, do community institutions treat citizens as producers? If so, a checkup could include looking for grassroots associations, the rate at which new ones are forming, and their relation to community institutions.

As evidence of the effectiveness of civic associations of all sizes and missions, recall the Sharkey study of the cities where crime had declined. And look again at the research on the importance of ad hoc groups that play a critical role in responding to disasters.[85] In these cases, citizens weren't simply carrying out the mission of a larger institution. So you might want to ask whether citizens are doing the things only citizens can do. What are they producing? Is what they produce being used by professionals and community institutions like hospitals, departments of public safety, and schools? Have schools, for example, found ways to incorporate into their curriculum what communities can do to educate?

## COMMUNICATIONS, CONNECTIONS, AND NETWORKS

Another characteristic of high-achieving communities is the *way* people are connected to one another. If the social bonds are restrictive, the connections can be oppressive. If they are too loose, a sense of community suffers; people feel alone and unsupported. "How and in what way is our community connected?" may be a revealing question to ask in a checkup.

**ANOTHER CHARACTERISTIC OF HIGH-ACHIEVING COMMUNITIES IS THE WAY PEOPLE ARE CONNECTED TO ONE ANOTHER.**

Resilience appears to have a great deal to do with the way information flows. In *Why the Garden Club Couldn't Save Youngstown*, Sean Safford compares the civic connections in two similar rust belt cities.[86] Both had been successful manufacturing centers until they experienced economic reversals in the late 1970s and early 1980s. One was more resilient and responded better. Why? The way communication flowed was a factor, as was the nature of the connections that people formed with one another. Communication and social capital or connection that join disparate parts of a community facilitate shared learning.

According to Safford, in the less resilient city, civic networks were organized somewhat like a wagon wheel with a central hub. Communication went to the central point and then back out. The more resilient city, on the other hand, was organized in multiple nodes, which promoted "interaction—

and mobilization—across social, political and economic divisions."[87] Anyone could get to most anyone else, which helped counter the exclusiveness of factions. Perhaps you will want to look at how your community is "wired."

Do most of the communications go to central hubs and then back out? Or does the pattern look more like a web with multiple nodes? In a web, communication flows in all directions. The internet is like this; everybody can usually connect to everybody else. This type of communication system fosters the growth of networks. The more networks there are connecting different groups and different parts of a community, the stronger that community is. Networks create what is called "bridging capital." You might look at networks and networking in your checkup.

A learning community has decentralized communications and multiple networks. Civic projects need not be centrally directed but can be connected through shared purposes, which makes them more likely to be mutually reinforcing.

A community culture that encourages numerous small initiatives that are connected provides greater opportunities for a community to change constructively than depending on one single initiative, which is susceptible to systems failure. A monocentric culture has only one central source of reliable information; a polycentric culture has multiple sources. The culture of a community influences communications patterns, which influence how change occurs. A monocentric culture changes by getting up to scale. A polycentric culture fosters changes by "infection" and by innovation. People learn from one another; innovation spreads. People in one neighborhood adapt what they see somewhere else to fit their own situation. This process isn't like getting up to scale.[88] Infection takes hold because "the action of one individual or a small group can affect the whole system very rapidly."[89] You might look at how change occurs in your community.

## WHAT'S NEXT?

Chapter 5 adds to the questions that might be used in a community checkup. It draws on what chapter 3 said about the influence of a deliberative environment on people learning together. This is the kind of learning that helps people discover ways of combining differences in perceptions and concerns without eliminating the differences.

CHAPTER FIVE

# CHECKING UP TO LEARN TOGETHER

This chapter continues the checkup begun in chapter 4. The questions suggested for your next conversations are intended to generate useful information on how your community goes about solving problems and enlisting those who may not usually be engaged in civic initiatives because they aren't sure that their time and effort will make a difference.

## GETTING STARTED

### *GATHERING CONCERNS*

What do people in your community consider deeply valuable? Although people don't usually have a prepared list of what is deeply important, they can often recall experiences that made them realize that some things are absolutely essential to their well-being. For instance, the COVID-19 pandemic made us appreciate the security provided by a caring and supportive community, which was illustrated by actions like neighbors dropping off groceries so others wouldn't have to go to crowded stores. Most people don't talk in abstractions about imperatives like security, but we show what is deeply important by the stories we tell about our experiences and how they made us feel. Members of your group might begin gathering concerns by telling stories to one another about why they became concerned about community problems. What did they think was at stake? What kept them up at night? These concerns tell us what is truly valuable.

Every day, people discuss their concerns, their hopes and fears. What I'm suggesting isn't some special technique; it is just doing what happens naturally in a more expeditious way and with a certain objective in mind—to identify the things that people in the community care deeply about. People are already motivated by their greatest concerns; recognizing what they are engages us.

Let me say more about the kinds of concerns that I'm talking about. I don't mean frustrations or pet peeves. I mean the things that really motivate people. These aren't what we think of today as "values." They are much older. I mentioned one earlier—security from danger. Human beings have always been motivated by such primal incentives for their survival. We have wanted to be secure from danger and have found that security by joining forces (collaborative efforts) to protect ourselves. These same survival instincts have made us want to be free from any type of coercion that would interfere with our ability to seek out new sources of food and water. And when our ancestors joined with others to hunt or gather food, they wanted to have an equitable share of what their collective efforts produced. Otherwise, those not receiving a fair share would leave the group, making it less effective in hunting and foraging. Most of all, human beings have been "programmed" to seek the control we need to be secure, free from coercion, and treated equitably. This primal programming still affects people today.

Questions to begin this conversation on concerns might be:

- What is the most serious problem our community faces?
- How does this problem affect you and your family?
- Do we know anyone who has different concerns?

[What questions have worked best for groups that have developed their own issue books? Are there other questions that might help here?]

## MOVING FORWARD

A conversation about concerns isn't for group therapy. It's the opening round in a problem-solving strategy that moves on to look at how problems are being described in the community. How are they being named? And by whom?

**WHO GETS TO "NAME" A PROBLEM AND HOW THEY NAME IT MAKE A POWERFUL DIFFERENCE IN PROBLEM SOLVING. DEFINING A PROBLEM OR GIVING IT A NAME DETERMINES THE NUMBER OF PEOPLE WHO WILL BE AVAILABLE TO COMBAT IT AND THE KIND OF RESPONSES THAT WILL EMERGE.**

## GIVING NAMES TO PROBLEMS

Who gets to "name" a problem and how they name it make a powerful difference in problem solving. Defining a problem or giving it a name determines the number of people who will be available to combat it and the kind of responses that will emerge. As Charles Kettering said, "A problem well-defined is a problem half-solved."[90]

As people become more aware of what is deeply valuable, they have taken the first step in naming problems. For example, to recognize that a pandemic is an issue of safety is to expand the definition of the problem from one of virology alone to one of being secure from danger.

Naming goes on every day in communities, though not always using people's terms. The news media are constantly naming problems, often using the language of partisan politics. Politicians know to select names that are favorable to their purposes. Experts and professionals use academic or scientific names. Advocates may use ideological language. None of these names are necessarily wrong, and citizens themselves sometimes use them. However, these names are different from the names that are rooted in people's concerns about what is deeply valuable. One way citizens can make a difference is by adding their names for problems to the community decision-making.

## WHAT ARE OUR OPTIONS?

If people are focused on what they hold dear and are talking about naming community problems in those terms, they are probably already thinking about possible actions to combat the problems. While there is a natural impatience to solve problems quickly, sound decisions require considering all reasonable options first. Identifying these options creates a helpful framework for community decision-making. Developing an issue framework puts a handle on problems that are so big and amorphous that practical solutions seem out of reach.

The options for action follow from the various things people consider deeply valuable. So, in the conversations with your fellow readers, you might ask questions like, "If you are concerned about X, what actions do you think would work?" You might set the stage for this conversation by reflecting on past decision-making that touched off "solution wars" or cases when potentially useful remedies were never considered.

The questions useful in creating a framework can be simple and direct. Often these questions spark conversations about where the resources needed to act can be found. (I'll say more about that shortly.)

Consider identifying one community issue that has received a good deal of consideration in your conversations about concerns and names. Then, think of at least three options for dealing with the problem that follow from what people said was deeply important. For each option, identify who needs to act.

What about citizens themselves as actors? The first response to the question about actors is likely to be about officials and institutions with the authority to act (mayors, elected representatives, and administrators like school superintendents).

A question about citizens themselves can be as straightforward as "What can we do ourselves?" What are some things people say that they would be willing to do personally to improve the community?

**RECOGNIZING TENSIONS:** As you look over the options based on what has been said about concerns, are there any tensions or costs and possibly negative consequences that need to be recognized? "If we do X, what if that hurts Y?" What happened in your conversation when you recognized the costs and trade-offs? What did you learn as you weighed the different options against the things you hold dear? Did all the options get a "fair trial" in your conversation? What about the least popular ones?

[These questions may not be phrased exactly as you would say them. We hope to learn from the questions you and others ask.]

Because people are influenced by a range of primal imperatives, it is inevitable, in different conditions, that these will conflict. For instance, if the situation is one in which there are serious questions about the behavior of some police and also the need to be safe from crime, the imperatives for fair treatment or justice can be in tension with the need to be secure from danger. Options for actions to reform policing will encounter options for ensuring public safety. Both are very valuable, and both have to be considered in community decision-making. But that requires recognizing that every option has costs and potentially undesirable consequences. On the positive side, recognizing tensions and trying to work through them as much as possible stimulates the movement from hasty, impulsive reactions to more shared and reflective judgment.

## WEIGHING OPTIONS TO DECIDE

Recall a time when you were faced with making a difficult personal choice, when there were several options, yet each had pros and cons to consider. In situations like this, people usually weigh the options as carefully as they can and then decide on a way to move forward. Even if they don't choose one of the options, they may find a way to balance the competing demands. For example, striking a balance might mean delaying one option until another has been implemented. Community institutions like town councils and school boards should be doing the same careful weighing in making decisions.

Once your group has selected an issue and created a framework of several options to consider, try working through the tensions, not necessarily to the point where everyone agrees, but to the point where you can see a way that the community can move forward in dealing with the problem you have selected.

**WORKING CONDITIONS:** In order for the decision-making to lead to sound judgment, participants should be aware of, and be willing to accept, certain preconditions. Everyone should be aware that they are going to hear opinions they don't like. Also, the objective isn't to get participants to change their minds or agree. It is to identify what the people in a community are and aren't willing to do in order to combat the problem being considered. This could lead to discovering ways for the community to move forward short of full agreement.

Some questions to discuss at this point in your conversations with others might be variations of these:

- Do we have all the options we should consider on the table?
- Are there some things people care deeply about, but we haven't crafted an option for acting? And what about people in the community who aren't here? What actions might address their concerns?
- If you heard something that you don't agree with, what might be a reason for the contrary opinion? Can you appreciate or understand the reason even if you don't agree with it?
- As we weighed the possible costs and negative consequences of our options, how did we come out? What happened?
- Recognizing our differences, but knowing we need to do something about the community problem we are focused on, are there steps that might improve our chances of finding a way forward?

[Are there questions that helped groups that hit an impasse?]

Note: The questions listed here aren't to be taken literally. There are better questions that you will think of that fit the conversation you are having.

## *LOCATING RESOURCES*

Thinking of options for action on a problem raises the question of who the actors should be, which leads to questions about what resources are needed. The matter of resources is inherent in the decision-making. Your checkup might usefully include resource questions.

The obvious resources, such as a city's budget, are going to be those of obviously powerful actors, such as the mayor or city manager. The less obvious answers may be about citizens with untapped resources. That's where you might uncover hidden treasures. Recall Chattanooga, where people made an inventory of all the places in town where young people could learn something. The schools certainly had resources, but so did museums, libraries, and barbershops. Your conversation here might use questions that would draw on people's imaginations. Other questions might be those that John McKnight used, which weren't about "resources." They were questions about the "gifts" (skills, experiences) people had that they would be willing to share.

## ORGANIZING COMPLEMENTARY ACTION

Inevitably, in conversations that identify numerous actors who have resources to offer, the attention will turn to questions about organization. Effective action usually requires some type of coordination. Typically, this is done through one central agency, a Square, with a bureaucracy capable of managing a multifaceted initiative.

Some type of coordination is needed for responding to problems with causes coming from all quarters of a community. There is no one institution or profession that can be effective in dealing with them. To avoid the unintended consequences of bureaucratic centralization, what kind of coordination can deal with a number of independent actors in different parts of a community?

**SELF-ORGANIZING:** Communities have many ways of organizing actions that don't require centralized management; your group might want to look into them. You could begin by checking into your own experiences. Have you ever seen an event that was organized without a central organizer in charge? What about a gathering that happened when somebody said, "Let's all meet at the coffee shop tomorrow morning"? Have you ever been to a potluck supper where there was no agreed-on menu and everyone just brought a favorite dish? Think about crowd sourcing online. All of these are examples of self-organizing. Consider looking for opportunities to perpetuate self-organizing by bringing people doing similar work together.

Self-organizing can also benefit from intentional civic "matchmaking." Look for potential partnerships. Find organizations that are willing to make introductions. Some foundations see that as part of their role in a community. Self-organizing can also follow from community forums where participants have discovered shared concerns and objectives. Are there civic efforts going on in your community that could be strengthened by reinforcement from other civic efforts? Where are there more opportunities for greater collaboration?

**ARE THERE CIVIC EFFORTS GOING ON IN YOUR COMMUNITY THAT COULD BE STRENGTHENED BY REINFORCEMENT FROM OTHER CIVIC EFFORTS? WHERE ARE THERE MORE OPPORTUNITIES FOR GREATER COLLABORATION?**

I'm not suggesting that all complementary action has to be self-organized. But this type of coordination is often overlooked.

### *EVALUATION AS LEARNING*

The usual way of evaluating a civic project is to bring in an outside authority who will measure tangible evidence of progress using objectives set when the project began. That has the advantage of having a presumably objective judge and being able to show tangible results. Many funders require such evaluations. However, there are additional ways of evaluating. They use community learning.

Of all the checkup questions, none are more important than those that deal with this learning. Optimally, your group has been learning about the community throughout your conversations. You can see what you've been learning by reviewing each set of questions that you've been talking about. What have you learned from concern gathering? From looking into who names the community's problems and how? From the way decisions are made, resources are identified, organizing is done and, now, how evaluations are conducted? (This review and your reflections will be very relevant when you get to chapter 7.)

You have been deliberating when you have been talking together about the questions in this chapter. Evaluating can be reflecting on what you've learned. It is deliberating in reverse because it begins by assessing what you have learned.

Here is a more complete list of checkup questions that you can use to evaluate what you've been learning:

- Is the problem we were focusing on really what we thought it was?
- Was the name we gave it the right one?
- Did we identify what was most valuable to people?
- Did what we thought was most important turn out to be right?
- Did we capture the tensions among the things we held valuable in the way we framed the issue?
- Did we work through the tensions? Did we give a fair trial to the most unpopular options for solving the problem?
- Did we come up with a general sense of purpose and direction, even if we didn't fully agree?
- Did we recognize and tap into all the resources we might have?
- Did the actions taken complement one another?
- Were there opportunities for self-organizing? Could more be created?

The purpose of learning together is to create a learning community. But there is no standardized test you can use to evaluate your community's progress. It is possible, however, to see whether a community is working in a deliberative mode. And deliberating isn't just weighing options carefully and fairly. It is also a way of learning together. The ancient Greeks called deliberation "the talk we use to teach ourselves before we act" (*logo prodidacthenai*).[91]

There are also other ways to know whether a community is learning. One way is to look at the amount of experimentation that is going on. Teachers might be trying new ways to teach. Local governments and NGOs could be testing ways of working *with*, not just *for*, citizens. New businesses might be opening. Is there a welcoming attitude toward trying new approaches to old problems?

**THE PURPOSE OF LEARNING TOGETHER IS TO CREATE A LEARNING COMMUNITY. BUT THERE IS NO STANDARDIZED TEST YOU CAN USE TO EVALUATE YOUR COMMUNITY'S PROGRESS. IT IS POSSIBLE, HOWEVER, TO SEE WHETHER A COMMUNITY IS WORKING IN A DELIBERATIVE MODE.**

## MOVING OUT

Hopefully, your conversations with other readers have been productive even though there may have been bumps along the way. That's often the case because the questions you've been asking yourselves aren't easy ones.

Of course, as you know, one conversation in one group isn't enough to affect the community-as-a-whole. You can begin to do that by inviting others to test the issue your group has named and framed. You can sponsor your own deliberative forum. This has been done in many communities with encouraging results. There are plenty of NIF veteran moderators who would be willing to help you.[92]

## WHAT'S NEXT?

At this point, readers probably want to know what it might look like in real life if a community tried a learning strategy. Chapter 6 paints a picture of life in such a community.

CHAPTER SIX

# REACHING OUT TO THE WHOLE COMMUNITY

As you are aware, the improvements you and your fellow readers hope for depend on citizens working together throughout the community. But how do you engage them when one of the things that concerns you is the lack of civic engagement? Passionate appeals to the common good, convincing evidence of a need, carefully reasoned arguments—none of these may have been enough to rouse the citizenry.

## THE COMMUNITY-AS-A-WHOLE

The last chapter made a point that you may already recognize. The work you have done in your group has to move out into your community in order to realize the benefits that you hope for. Whatever you hope will happen can begin in a small group. That is where most progress begins. "Never doubt," anthropologist Margaret Mead said, "that a small group of thoughtful, committed citizens can change the world." And some believe she added, "Indeed, it is the only thing that ever has."[93] If she didn't add that, maybe she should have, even though there are many other forces that bring about change. My point here isn't about who said what. It's about using what you've done to reach throughout your community.

If you are in a group reading this book, it's essential that you first test the checkup questions among yourselves. It is also essential that you test them with the citizens you hope will be more engaged. How and where that is done depends on circumstances in your community that only you would know.

Obviously, the first decision that other citizens have to make is whether to participate. Often that takes having the experience of "trying on" deliberation to see whether it fits. This can be done in a forum, using the issue that you have named and framed. Then those who have benefited from that experience can gather their own concerns, give a name to an issue that concerns them, and produce a framework for their own deliberative forums. Those are the elements of a learning strategy.

## THE SUGGSVILLE STORY

When you reach this point in the book, you may feel the need for an example of what using a learning strategy might look like in real life. Although sacrificing some of the authenticity of individual stories, Kettering created a composite town—an avatar—called Suggsville to show what can happen when a small group's efforts have an impact throughout a community.[94] We based the Suggsville composite on things we had seen actually occur, though in different places and times. And not wanting to claim that the foundation had found perfect communities to use as models, we drew from communities we had seen that were less than ideal. We wanted to show the difficulties citizens encounter in doing their work.

Suggsville was, and still is, rural and poor. Once a prosperous farming community, the town began to decline during the 1970s as the agricultural economy floundered. By the 1990s, the unemployment rate soared above 40 percent. Property values plummeted. With little else to replace the income from idle farms, a drug trade flourished. A majority of Suggsville's babies were being born to single teenagers. The schools were plagued with low test scores and troubling dropout rates. Chronic disease rates were higher than in most communities; obesity was becoming an epidemic, and alcoholism was pervasive. Although people had lived together for generations, the community was divided economically and racially. Nearly everyone who could leave the town had, especially college-educated young adults. Overwhelmed by these difficulties, many people doubted their ability to do anything that would make a difference.

## NAMING PROBLEMS

After church services and in the one grocery store that survived, Suggsvillians discussed with friends and neighbors what was happening in their town. Different clusters made small talk and mulled over the town's difficulties, but no decisions were made or actions taken. Then consultants from the state land-grant university who had been asked to advise a small group of civic leaders made a modest suggestion—begin town meetings where citizens could assess their situation and decide what they might do. The group's first meeting drew the predictable handful. And they sat in racially homogeneous clusters—until someone rearranged the chairs into a circle and people began to mingle. After participants got off their favorite soapboxes and stopped looking for others to blame, they settled down to identifying the problems that concerned everyone. Economic security was at the top of the list, though it wasn't the only concern. Crime was another.

As the town meetings continued—slowly, sometimes haltingly—Suggsvillians named several problems, which reflected the things they valued. People didn't choose one issue and discard all the others. Restoring economic well-being resonated with other concerns like family instability. The social structure and moral order also seemed to be crumbling, and people felt insecure.

As people added names for problems, they implicated themselves in solving them. They could do something about the alcoholism that was threatening both families and the social order. And they could do something about the children who suffered when adults took little responsibility for their well-being. Naming problems as people experienced them was the first step in citizens regaining a sense of being able to make a difference.

**NAMING PROBLEMS AS PEOPLE EXPERIENCED THEM WAS THE FIRST STEP IN CITIZENS REGAINING A SENSE OF BEING ABLE TO MAKE A DIFFERENCE.**

## *FRAMING ISSUES WITH THE TENSIONS SHOWING*

Given concerns about the economy, one of the first proposals in what had become a series of Suggsville town meetings was to recruit a manufacturing company. This option stayed on the table although some participants had a practical objection: Every other town in the state was competing for new industries. Some people favored a grow-your-own strategy. Maybe several small businesses could expand. But not convinced that this was a good option, a few who felt strongly about recruiting new industry left the group and went to the state office of economic development for assistance. Nonetheless, the majority of the participants continued to discuss the option of encouraging local businesses. Several mentioned a restaurant that had opened recently; it promised to stimulate a modest revival downtown. Unfortunately, that promise wasn't being realized because unemployed men (and youngsters who liked to hang out with them) were congregating on the street in front of the restaurant drinking beer. Customers shied away.

At this point in the Suggsville meetings, having heard most everyone's concerns and the options for possible actions, there was an opportunity to create an inclusive framework for the decisions needed to make visions into realities. The options were to attract outside business, "grow your own," or turn the problem over to the state development agency. Attracting outside business could provide economic security, but the business might bring automation—robots directed not by local workers but by skilled employees from out of town. People valued the security, that a local workforce would provide, yet they also saw value in exploring new economic frontiers like automation. "Growing your own" by building on existing small businesses had a lot of appeal. People knew and trusted the local entrepreneurs. There was also security in that, and it would give the community more control. However, there were fears that local businesses, once they were profitable, would be bought up by outside conglomerates. That would end local control. Turning the economic problem over to experts in the state government offered the security of having knowledgeable professionals in charge. But the "cost" to local control would be substantial. Every option considered was attractive because it resonated with what people valued, yet each had costs and unattractive consequences that also threatened other things people held dear. There were tensions throughout all the options.

## *DELIBERATING TO DECIDE*

At the next Suggsville meeting, attendance was higher. Some members of the town council and a few other officials came. Participants knew what was at stake: nothing less than the life of the community. In a forum on what to do, Suggsvillians began talking about the grow-your-own option using the new restaurant as an example. Initially, the conversation was about whom to blame for the restaurant's difficulties. The police chief argued that the problem was loitering and recommended stricter enforcement of ordinances. Others weren't so sure. Strict enforcement, even if it worked to clear the streets, could give the community the feel of a police state. Could people live with these consequences? Those being blamed thought about dropping out of the meetings.

Still others worried about problems they thought contributed to the loitering. One woman suggested that loitering was symptomatic of widespread alcoholism. As citizens put their concerns on the table, they struggled with what was most important to the welfare of the community. People valued a great many things. The Suggsville that they hoped to create would be family friendly and safe for kids. It would have good schools as well as a strong economy.

Yet everything that would have to be done to reach those objectives had potential downsides, as was the case with stricter law enforcement. Once again, tensions were unavoidable. People had to decide what was really most valuable to the community. They seemed ready to weigh the potential consequences of different options against the things they held dear.

### IDENTIFYING AND COMMITTING RESOURCES

As people in Suggsville were working through tensions, some civic groups were already taking action or planning to. Deciding and acting were intertwined. Worried that too many youngsters had too little adult supervision, several community organizations responded with offers of things they were willing to do if others would join them: organize baseball and softball leagues, provide after-school classes, expand youth services in the churches, form a band. The observation that alcoholism was contributing to the town's difficulties prompted others in the meetings to propose that a chapter of Alcoholics Anonymous (AA) be established. Where would it meet? Someone offered a vacant building free of charge. As more projects developed and citizens called on others to join them, new recruits began coming to the meetings. Rather than deciding on a single solution, people mounted an array of initiatives that were loosely coordinated because the initiatives were reasonably consistent with the sense of direction that was emerging from the deliberations.

## ORGANIZING COMPLEMENTARY ACTING

As civic work in Suggsville progressed, several people returned to the argument that, while encouraging local businesses was fine, it would never provide enough jobs to revive the economy. The town still had to attract outside investment, they insisted. Someone quickly pointed out that the center of town, especially the park, was so unsightly that no one of sound mind would consider Suggsville an attractive location for a new business. Even though several saw little connection between the condition of the park and recruiting industry, no one denied that the town needed a facelift. Suggsville's three-member sanitation crew, however, had all it could do to keep up with garbage collection. Did people feel strongly enough about the cleanup to accept the implications? Would they show up to clean the park themselves? In the past, responses to similar calls had been minimal. This time, after one of the community forums, a group of people agreed to gather at the park the following Saturday with rakes, mowers, and trash bags.

During most of these meetings, the recently elected mayor sat quietly, keeping an eye on what was happening. The community forums had begun during his predecessor's administration, and the town's new leader felt no obligation to them. In fact, he was a bit suspicious of what the participants were doing. Members of the town council feared the public meetings would result in just another pressure group. But no one made any demands on the town government, although some citizens thought it strange that the mayor hadn't offered to help with the cleanup. Then, when Saturday arrived, people were surprised to find that the mayor sent workers to the park with trucks and other heavy equipment to do what the tools brought from home couldn't.

The cleanup of the park was probably what prompted an effort to restore the oldest cemetery, which was in the historical district. People didn't just remove weeds and debris, they brought relics from their homes to honor their ancestors: a flower urn that had belonged to one of the early settlers, even a bust of the first mayor that had been lovingly fashioned by a grandson. The town's maintenance department didn't have memorabilia like these; only the families could have made the cemetery more than just a graveyard. Their contributions made the cemetery unique, which encouraged pilgrimages from former residents. Their visits were an added boost to the revitalization initiatives. History was a resource.

## LEARNING AS A COMMUNITY

In time, the ad hoc Suggsville improvement group holding the forums became an official civic association. As might be expected, the organization had the usual internal disputes that detracted from community problem solving. Still, when a controversy was brewing or an emerging issue needed to be addressed, the association was there to bring people together.

Some projects didn't work. In most instances, when that happened, association members adjusted their sights and launched more initiatives. Perhaps this momentum had something to do with the way the association involved the community in evaluating projects. The association regularly convened meetings where citizens could reflect on what the community had learned, regardless of whether the projects succeeded. Success wasn't as important as the lessons that could be used in future efforts.

**CITIZENS COULD REFLECT ON WHAT THE COMMUNITY HAD LEARNED, REGARDLESS OF WHETHER THE PROJECTS SUCCEEDED. SUCCESS WASN'T AS IMPORTANT AS THE LESSONS THAT COULD BE USED IN FUTURE EFFORTS.**

## WHAT HAPPENED?

Although the restaurant held its own, new industry didn't come to Suggsville. Drug traffic continued to be a problem, yet people's vigilance, together with more surveillance by the police department, reduced the trade. The crowd loitering on the streets dwindled away. More people attended the AA meetings even though alcoholism remained a challenge. A new summer recreation program became popular with young people, and teenage pregnancies decreased a bit, as did the high school dropout rate.

Attendance at the Suggsville association meetings continued to rise and fall, depending on which problems were being addressed. Some association members worried about these fluctuations; yet others concentrated on building ties with civic groups and rural neighborhood coalitions, as well as with institutions like the county law enforcement agencies, the state's economic development office, and the public health department. Creating networks became a priority. Several people dropped out because they wanted the association to play a more partisan role. But the association refused to get drawn into local election campaigns or to endorse special causes.

Suggsville wouldn't make anyone's list of model communities; still, the town had changed: Citizens had a greater ability to influence their future. Asked what the years of civic work produced, one Suggsvillian said it was learning how to work together better. That, in itself, made Suggsville a better place to live.

## WHAT'S NEXT?

Even though Suggsville is a composite, everything described is based on real life. (There is a cemetery with locally made art near where I grew up.) While there was no discussion of anything called a "learning strategy," people in the town forums were learning anew about themselves and their community. The small group of civic leaders and, later, the civic association, provided opportunities for that to occur. It took time, but the instigators were patient. Providing opportunities for people to learn together as they act together is admittedly an unorthodox strategy for strengthening communities, yet it may appeal to people's willingness to experiment with new ways of working together.

**PROVIDING OPPORTUNITIES FOR PEOPLE TO LEARN TOGETHER AS THEY ACT TOGETHER IS ADMITTEDLY AN UNORTHODOX STRATEGY FOR STRENGTHENING COMMUNITIES, YET IT MAY APPEAL TO PEOPLE'S WILLINGNESS TO EXPERIMENT WITH NEW WAYS OF WORKING TOGETHER.**

Chapter 7's purpose is to help communities stimulate more civic innovation within and around them. It does that by providing space for readers to make a record of what they have learned and to imagine what they could do moving forward.

CHAPTER SEVEN

# YOUR STORY

This is the chapter with mostly blank pages. We wanted to provide space for you and the other readers to make a record of what you have learned and what you hope to learn going forward. You can find out a great deal by reflecting on what you have done. It doesn't have to be a success story. Actually, it will be better if, rather than focusing on the success or failure of your efforts, chapter 7 is a candid account of what you struggled with and anything you discovered as a result. Learning communities are inventive, and inventors find out how to fail successfully.

Your story is also very important because it can help launch new initiatives in your community and perhaps in others.

## YOUR JOURNAL

What you write on the blank pages might resemble a diary or journal. This journal can be useful, for example, in capturing what happened and what you learned by taking a fresh look at how problems were named and how decisions were made in your community. Producing something concrete like a journal might help make learning together less abstract.

The journal should be produced by the group itself. Writing a journal can help people sort out what they have learned about their community and their role in it. Here are some questions you might adapt in preparing such a journal:

- What did the self-diagnostic checkups show? What did we think might be done to strengthen the community so it could work more effectively and democratically?
- What wicked problems did we identify, and what did we think needed to be done to combat them?
- In selecting an issue to focus on, what did we learn about what was deeply valuable to people?
- Were there related issues that needed to be framed for future community deliberation?

- What was learned from the deliberative forums?
- What actions were identified? Who accepted responsibility for implementing them?
- What untapped resources were identified? What needed to happen so people would become more aware of their assets?
- What needed to be done to strengthen networks and decenter communication?
- Where were there opportunities for complementary acting?
- Where did we see that collaboration could be increased?

These are all questions for evaluating what you've done.

## DEVELOPING SCENARIOS FOR THE FUTURE

Writing a journal might also include imagining a series of steps that would show how your community could move forward to combat problems with wicked characteristics. Laying out these steps might be called creating a "scenario," which is a coherent narrative connecting the steps you will take to continue the work you've begun.

Scenario building to identify work that needs to go forward is necessary because the wickedness of some problems moves forward too. It is never-ending; so efforts to respond have to be ongoing. One forum on one issue won't be enough. One project, even if it lasts a year, won't be enough. A community has to keep learning and acting.

Your scenario might also include steps you would take to work with groups in other parts of your community so they can gather their own concerns and then name and frame issues for deliberation. These other groups could get started by participating in one of your forums.

### *MAKING COVENANTS*

Who is going to do the work that these scenarios lay out? Who has the necessary resources? Who will accept responsibility? What will ensure that people and organizations will actually do what they say they will? One way people have answered these questions is by making mutual promises to do what needs doing. (Recall the people in Suggsville who pledged to organize an AA group if someone would provide a meeting space.) Mutual promises tap into the power of reciprocity. "If you will do X, we will do Y." If these pledges are made publicly, they become covenants, and covenants have a history that's worth recalling.

While covenants aren't legal contracts, they have been effective throughout history. In this country, the famous Mayflower Compact is an example. That was a voluntary agreement among settlers about how the Plymouth Colony would operate. Covenants are effective because they are made in the presence of other people. Social pressure promotes keeping these promises. The expectations of others can influence behavior when there are no laws or contracts to ensure compliance. A covenant is a pledge to take certain actions that will complement or support one another. These complementary actions make the whole of an initiative greater than the sum of its parts.

## A COMMUNITY OF COMMUNITIES

Now, it's time to set down your story. But before you turn to the blank journal pages, take a moment to recognize the opportunity ahead of you.

Our country needs strong communities. And although they compete in the economic arena (and in sports), they also help one another (for instance, when disaster strikes). In addition, they can profit by learning from one another and discovering new ways of engaging their citizens in the work that only citizens can do. The story you record here can benefit not only your own community, but other communities as well. It can help create a community of communities, which will help strengthen our democracy. Democracies well up and wane like the tides; still, they are incredibly resilient. You and your group can be a force in making our communities better and stronger.

## WHAT WE HAVE BEEN LEARNING

## ENDNOTES

1. The research and writing for this book began almost a decade ago in a different political climate. We live now in a much more contentious, divisive time. One of the characteristics of this climate is disagreement about the meaning and use of many of the terms found on these pages. Words like *citizen*, *community*, even *democracy* are now contested. And there doesn't appear to be any language that will not offend someone, for what they consider valid reasons. So those who helped me with the research and I acknowledge that some of the words used here have contested meanings. And we try to be as clear as we can about what we mean by the words we use and why we use them.
2. During the 2020 pandemic, some institutions in public health and public education did a bit better in the polls. Nonetheless, confidence in most authoritative institutions remained significantly below 50 percent. Gallup Poll, *Amid Pandemic, Confidence in Key U.S. Institutions Surges*, August 12, 2020, https://news.gallup.com /poll/317135/amid-pandemic-confidence-key-institutions-surges.aspx.
3. See, for example, Katherine J. Cramer, *The Politics of Resentment: Rural Consciousness in Wisconsin and the Rise of Scott Walker* (University of Chicago Press, 2016); Arlie Russell Hochschild, *Strangers in Their Own Land: Anger and Mourning on the American Right* (New York: New Press, 2016); Michael J. Sandel, *The Tyranny of Merit: What's Become of the Common Good?* (New York: Farrar, Straus & Giroux, 2020).
4. Thomas Hobbes, *Leviathan*, ed. C. B. Macpherson (New York: Penguin Books, 1968), 185.
5. See the reporting and survey results of the Hidden Common Ground initiative, a collaboration among Public Agenda, IPSOS, USA TODAY, America Amplified public radio network, the National Issues Forums, and the Kettering Foundation, https://www.usatoday.com hiddencommonground; https://www.publicagenda.org/programs-reports/the-hidden-common-ground-initiative; and https//www.nifi.org/en/hidden-common-ground.
6. See, for example, Janet Adamy, "Abortion, Guns and Trump: A Church Group Tries to Navigate America's Divisions," *Wall Street Journal*, December 18, 2020, https://www.wsj.com/articles/abortion-guns-and-trump-a-church-group-tries-to-navigate-americas-divisions-11608298552.

7. The foundation has an earlier publication, a well-received report titled *For Communities to Work* (Dayton, OH: Kettering Foundation Press, 2002). However, that research is now out of date, and we have new insights to share. This publication is a major update of that report.
8. James Traub, "Think Locally, Act Locally," review of *The Ordinary Virtues*, by Michael Ignatieff, Sunday Book Review, *New York Times,* October 15, 2017.
9. David Brooks, "The American Renaissance Is Underway," *New York Times,* May 15, 2018.
10. James Fallows, "The Reinvention of America," *Atlantic* (May 2018), https://www.theatlantic.com/magazine/ archive/2018/05/reinventing-america/556856/.
11. James Fallows and Deborah Fallows, *Our Towns: A 100,000-Mile Journey into the Heart of America* (New York: Pantheon Books, 2018).
12. Thomas L. Friedman, "Where American Politics Can Still Work: From the Bottom Up," *New York Times*, July 4, 2018.
13. Cary Funk, "Polling Shows Signs of Public Trust in Institutions amid the Pandemic," Pew Research Center, April 7, 2020, https://www.pewresearch.org/science/2020/04/07/polling-shows-signs-of-public-trust-in-institutions-amid-pandemic/.
14. This title was inspired by the 1973 classic by E. F. Schumacher.
15. Peter Block, *Community: The Structure of Belonging,* 2nd ed. (Oakland, CA: Berrett-Koehler Publishers, 2018), 98.
16. John McKnight, *The Four-Legged Stool* (Dayton, OH: Kettering Foundation, 2013).
17. Bobby Milstein, *Hygeia's Constellation: Navigating Health Futures in a Dynamic and Democratic World* (Atlanta: Centers for Disease Control and Prevention, April 15, 2008), 54–57.
18. The actual quote was: "I want to go back among our people, where they know when a man's sick, and they care when he dies." The father was in the hospital and asked LBJ to take him home. LBJ reminded him that he would get better medical care in the hospital and that was his father's response. Robert A. Caro, *The Passage of Power: The Years of Lyndon Johnson* (New York: Alfred A. Knopf, 2012), 146.
19. See Ronald A. Heifetz and Riley M. Sinder, "Political Leadership: Managing the Public's Problem Solving," in *The Power of Public Ideas*, ed. Robert B. Reich (Cambridge, MA: Ballinger Publishing,

1988), 185-191. See also subsequent writing by Heifetz on adaptive leadership.

20. Kurt Lewin, "Group Decision and Social Change," in *Readings in Social Psychology*, eds. G. E. Swanson, T. M. Newcomb, and E. L. Hartley (New York: Henry Holt and Company, 1952), 459-473.

21. Kurt Lewin's research showed that collective decision-making can change behavior and is more effective than moral appeals or "educating" the public with information. Lewin, "Group Decision and Social Change."

22. The prize was for the second book in a three-volume series. Lawrence Cremin, *American Education: The Colonial Experience, 1607-1783* (New York: Harper and Row, 1970); *American Education: The National Experience, 1783-1876* (New York: HarperCollins, 1980); and *American Education: The Metropolitan Experience 1876-1980* (New York: HarperCollins, 1988).

23. This was the definition used by Lawrence Cremin in the second book of his three-volume history of American education. Cremin, *American Education: The National Experience*, ix.

24. Cremin, *American Education: The Colonial Experience*; Cremin, *American Education: The National Experience*; and Cremin, *American Education: The Metropolitan Experience.*

25. See Jack Shelton, *Consequential Learning: A Public Approach to Better Schools* (Montgomery, AL: NewSouth Books, 2005), 51–58, 69–70, 80–91, 100–109.

26. Studies done by PACERS showed that while students from small, rural schools like the one in Coffeeville might not do so well in the beginning of their college careers, they did much better than students from larger schools by graduation. That is a vote for the value of small schools and of their communities. See Shelton, *Consequential Learning.*

27. Shelton, *Consequential Learning.*

28. See a study of citizens who aren't professional educators but who nonetheless teach, in Patricia Moore Harbour, *Community Educators: A Resource for Educating and Developing Our Youth* (Dayton, OH: Kettering Foundation Press, 2012).

29. Harbour, *Community Educators.*

30. Connie Crockett, "Communities as Educators: A Report on the November 2007 Public and Public Education Workshop,"

*Connections* (2008): 22–24. Also see Merlene Davis, "Beloved Bluegrass-Aspendale Teen Center a Casualty of Budget Cuts," *Lexington Herald-Leader*, May 22, 2011, https://www.kentucky.com/news/localcommunity /article44097090.htm/.

31. Another such program, in Springfield, Ohio, encourages kids to submit book reports to neighborhood barbershops and beauty salons. And barbershopbooks.org offers to send books to participating barbershops and train barbers to help kids learn to read. See "Cutting Illiteracy," which is an initiative of Conscious Connect, Inc. See http://theconsciousconnect.org/ and https://barbershopbooks.org.

32. Robert M. Cornett, "Reclaiming Our Children's Learning—A Strategy" (unpublished paper, Kettering Foundation archives, Dayton, OH, 2006).

33. Cornett, "Reclaiming Our Children's Learning." Other community resources used to educate include a bluegrass festival and a project to reintroduce chestnut trees into the Appalachian Mountains. The efforts involved a great many adults who were neither teachers nor parents.

34. Doble Research Associates, *Take Charge Workshop Series: Descriptions and Findings from the Field* (Dayton, OH: Report to the Kettering Foundation, 1993), 3. The Doble report found that asking people to "map the places of learning in their community has proven to be a very powerful and transformative exercise."

35. See Heather Harding, "Supplementary Education: Educating and Developing the Whole Child, An Interview with Edmund W. Gordon," Understanding Educational Equity and Excellence at Scale (A Project of the Annenberg Institute for School Reform at Brown University, January 2007).

36. Harding, "Supplementary Education."

37. John Doble, memorandum to Damon Higgins and Randa Slim, "Report on CERI Community Leadership Workshop Baton Rouge, LA, 6/23/93," July 19, 1993, 4.

38. J. Mac Holladay, *Economic and Community Development: A Southern Exposure* (Dayton, OH: Kettering Foundation, 1992), 7.

39. Francis Fukuyama, *Trust: The Social Virtues and the Creation of Prosperity* (New York: Free Press Paperbacks, 1995).

40. Vaughn L. Grisham Jr., *Tupelo: The Evolution of a Community*

(Dayton, OH: Kettering Foundation Press, 1999).

41. Susan Willey, *"Bitter Roots & Sweet Fruits": Tupelo Conversations and Memories* (Dayton, OH: Kettering Foundation, 1999).

42. The Kettering Foundation's 2020 report *With the People* is focused on what might be accomplished if our governing institutions worked more *with* the people.

43. Monica Schoch-Spana et al., "Community Engagement: Leadership Tool for Catastrophic Health Events," *Biosecurity and Bioterrorism: Biodefense Strategy, Practice, and Science* 5, no. 1 (2007): 10-11.

44. Patrick Sharkey, *Uneasy Peace: The Great Crime Decline, the Renewal of City Life, and the Next War on Violence* (New York: W. W. Norton, 2018).

45. Richard Florida, "The Great Crime Decline and the Comeback of Cities," Citylab, January 16, 2018, https://www.citylab.com/life/2018/01/the-great-crime-decline-and-the-comeback-of-cities/549998/.

46. Florida, "The Great Crime Decline."

47. Emily Badger, "The Unsung Role That Ordinary Citizens Played in the Great Crime Decline," The Upshot, *New York Times*, November 9, 2017, https://nyti.ms/2hlT3Mu.

48. John P. Kretzmann and John L. McKnight, *Building Communities from the Inside Out: A Path Toward Finding and Mobilizing a Community's Assets* (Evanston, IL: Center for Urban Affairs and Policy Research, Neighborhood Innovations Network, Northwestern University, 1993), 13-27.

49. John L. McKnight, "A Twenty-First Century Map for Healthy Communities and Families" (Evanston, IL: Institute for Policy Research, Northwestern University, 1996).

50. John P. Kretzmann, John L. McKnight, and Nicol Turner, "Voluntary Associations in Low-Income Neighborhoods: An Unexplored Community Resource" (Evanston, IL: Asset-Based Community Development Institute, Institute for Policy Research, Northwestern University, 1996).

51. Edgar S. Cahn, *No More Throw-Away People: The Co-Production Imperative*, 2nd ed. (Washington, DC: Essential Books, 2004). "The Parable of the Blobs and Squares" can be viewed at https://www.kettering.org/ blogs/parable-blobs-and-squares.

52. Cahn, *No More Throw-Away People*, 83–84.
53. Elinor Ostrom, "Covenanting, Co-Producing, and the Good Society," *PEGS* (Committee on the Political Economy of the Good Society) *Newsletter* 3, no. 2 (Summer 1993): 8.
54. Doble Research Associates, *How People Connect: The Public and Public Schools* (Dayton, OH: Report to the Kettering Foundation, June 1998), 5.
55. "American Democracy: Building the Perfect Citizen," *Economist* (August 20, 1998). Interestingly, in 2020, the *Economist* featured an article stating that "panels of ordinary people can solve problems that the professionals fear to tackle." See "Amateurs to the Rescue: Politicians Should Take Citizens' Assemblies Seriously," *Economist* (September 19, 2020), https://www.economist.com/leaders/2020/09/17/politicians-should-take-citizens-assemblies-seriously.
56. Shared knowledge is different from the valuable knowledge that is produced by scientific reasoning. This knowledge is based on experiences and understanding what those experiences mean to different people. This doesn't invalidate or replace fact-finding but rather complements it. Shared knowledge adds a human dimension to objective, impersonal knowledge. It is intentionally subjective.
57. Steven Sloman and Philip Fernbach, *The Knowledge Illusion* (New York: Riverhead Books, 2017), 206-207, 210-211.
58. Suzanne W. Morse, *Smart Communities: How Citizens and Local Leaders Can Use Strategic Thinking to Build a Brighter Future* (San Francisco: Jossey-Bass, 2004).
59. To read more about evolutionary theories on human decision-making, see Sloman and Fernbach, *The Knowledge Illusion*; and Yuval Noah Harari, *Sapiens: A Brief History of Humankind* (New York: Harper, 2015).
60. You can find out about Common Ground for Action at www.nifi.org/en/common-ground-action. Or, contact the National Issues Forums Institute at (800) 433-7834 or nifi@nifi.org.
61. Jay Theis, who teaches at Lone Star College, described this forum in an interview with the Kettering Foundation, https://vimeo.com/361298696. Maura Casey also writes about this forum in a blog on the Kettering Foundation website, https://www.kettering.org/blogs/six-college-campuses.

62. Kim Strandberg, Staffan Himmelroos, and Kimmo Grönlund, "Do Discussions in Like-Minded Groups Necessarily Lead to More Extreme Opinions? Deliberative Democracy and Group Polarization," *International Political Science Review* (June 26, 2017), https://journals.sagepub.com/doi/pdf/10.1177/0192512117692136.
63. Bonnie Braun et al., *Engaging Unheard Voices: Under What Conditions Can, and Will, Limited Resource Citizens Engage in the Deliberative Public Policy Process?* (College Park, MD: Report to the Kettering Foundation, March 2006), 5.
64. Horst W. J. Rittel and Melvin M. Webber, "Dilemmas in a General Theory of Planning," *Policy Sciences*, vol. 4, no. 2 (1973): 155-169.
65. This statement, attributed to Daniel Yankelovich, is often referred to as the McNamara fallacy, named for Robert McNamara, US Secretary of Defense from 1961-1968. The concept relates to what happens when decisions are made and based solely on quantitative observations—such as decisions made by the Secretary of Defense during the Vietnam War.
66. Jean Johnson, *Will It Be on the Test?: A Closer Look at How Leaders and Parents Think About Accountability in the Public Schools* (Public Agenda and Kettering Foundation, 2013).
67. Sheila A. Arens, *Examining the Meaning of Accountability: Reframing the Construct* (Aurora, CO: Mid-continent Research for Education and Learning, July 2005).
68. Johnson, *Will It Be on the Test?*, and Arens, *Examining the Meaning of Accountability*.
69. This argument was made by Ostrom in "Covenanting, Co-Producing, and the Good Society," 8.
70. Kettering has drawn a great deal from "Dilemmas in a General Theory of Planning," by Rittel and Webber. But the foundation has also drawn from its own research, so its understanding of "wickedness" is not exactly the same.
71. Einstein's story was of a blind beetle walking along on a curved twig. To the bug, the twig is straight. Mamardashvili tells of a squirrel who falls out of a tree.
72. This story comes from September 2018 conversations with Kent Spellman, executive director of the West Virginia Community Development Hub.
73. For one of the more complete accounts of new types of organizations, see Ori Brafman and Rod A. Beckstrom, *The Starfish and the Spider:*

*The Unstoppable Power of Leaderless Organizations* (New York: Penguin Press, 2006).

74. Myles Horton and Paulo Freire, *We Make the Road by Walking: Conversations on Education and Social Change* (Philadelphia: Temple University Press, 1991), 125-127.

75. Kipling calls triumph and disaster "two imposters" in his poem "If—." Rudyard Kipling, *A Choice of Kipling's Verse*, ed. T. S. Eliot (NY: Faber & Faber, 1954).

76. Grisham, *Tupelo*.

77. Grisham, *Tupelo*.

78. The foundation continues to see the importance of the widely dispersed, entrepreneurial leadership that was identified by The Harwood Group in *Forming Public Capital: Observations from Two Communities* (Dayton, OH: Report to the Kettering Foundation, August 1995), 5. To read more about Harwood's community research, see Richard C. Harwood, *Unleashed: A Proven Way Communities Can Spread Change and Make Real Hope for All* (Dayton, OH: Kettering Foundation Press, 2021). See also Suzanne W. Morse's chapter, "Growing New Leaders," in *Smart Communities*, 149–166.

79. Woodrow Wilson, speech at the Workingman's Dinner, New York, September 4, 1912.

80. Henrik Ibsen, *An Enemy of the People* (New York: Dover Publications, 1999), 9.

81. Robert J. Sampson, *Great American City: Chicago and the Enduring Neighborhood Effect* (Chicago: University of Chicago Press, 2012), 222.

82. For a deeper look into the concept of leaderfulness, see David Mathews, *Leaders or Leaderfulness? Lessons from High-Achieving Communities* (Dayton, OH: Kettering Foundation, 2016).

83. Kretzmann, McKnight, and Turner, "Voluntary Associations in Low-Income Neighborhoods."

84. McKnight, "A Twenty-First Century Map for Healthy Communities and Families."

85. You'll recall the studies, mentioned in chapter 1: Schoch-Spana et al., "Community Engagement"; and Sharkey, *Uneasy Peace*.

86. Sean Safford, *Why the Garden Club Couldn't Save Youngstown: The*

*Transformation of the Rust Belt* (Cambridge, MA: Harvard University Press, 2009).

87. Sean Safford, *Why the Garden Club Couldn't Save Youngstown: Civic Infrastructure and Mobilization in Economic Crises*, IPC Working Paper Series (Cambridge, MA: MIT, March 2004), 2. Safford later published this research in the book *Why the Garden Club Couldn't Save Youngstown*.

88. McKnight, *The Four-Legged Stool*.

89. Carne Ross, *The Leaderless Revolution: How Ordinary People Will Take Power and Change Politics in the 21st Century* (New York: Blue Rider Press, 2011), xvii.

90. While this statement has been widely attributed to Charles Kettering, it has also been attributed to John Dewey. We have been unable to locate the source of the statement, but because it fits with Charles Kettering's approach to research and invention, I have included it here. This quote is sometimes worded as, "A problem well-stated is a problem half-solved."

91. See Robert Beekes, *Etymological Dictionary of Greek*, vol. 1 (Boston: Leiden, 2010), 325, 772; and Henry Liddell and Robert Scott, eds., *A Greek-English Lexicon* (Oxford: Clarendon Press, 1968), 386-387, 992.

92. To get in touch with experienced forum moderators, contact the National Issues Forums Institute via email at nifi@nifi.org.

93. This quote has long been attributed to Margaret Mead and is now trademarked by The Institute for Intercultural Studies. The institute, which was established by Mead in 1944, states: "Although the Institute has received many inquiries about this famous admonition by Margaret Mead, we have been unable to locate when and where it was first cited. . . . We believe it probably came into circulation through a newspaper report of something said spontaneously and informally. We know, however, that it was firmly rooted in her professional work and that it reflected a conviction that she expressed often, in different contexts and phrasings." More can be found at http://www.intercultural studies.org/faq.html.

94. The Suggsville story is drawn from more than 50 communities. These include Tupelo, Mississippi, as described by Grisham in *Tupelo*; and Uniontown, Alabama, as described by Joe A. Sumners, with Christa Slaton and Jeremy Arthur, in *Building Community: The Uniontown Story* (Dayton, OH: Report to the Kettering Foundation, 2005). Also see *For Communities to Work*.